Own the Forest, Delegate the Trees

Barbara V. Pratt

www.ProjectLeadershipGold.com

OWN THE FOREST, DELEGATE THE TREES. Copyright 2008 by Barbara V. Pratt. All rights reserved. Printed in the United States of America. Except as permitted under the United Sates Copyright Act of 1976, no part of this publication may be reproduced or distributed in any form or by any means, or stored in a data base or retrieval system, without prior written permission of the publisher.

This publication is to provide accurate and authoritative information in regard to the subject matter covered. It is sold with the understanding that neither the author nor the publisher is engaged in rendering legal, accounting, or other professional service. If legal advice or other expert assistance is required, the services of a competent professional person should be sought.

— *from a Declaration of Principles jointly adopted by a Committee of the American Bar Association and a Committee of Publishers*

ATTENTION CORPORATIONS & ORGANIZATIONS

This book is available at a special discount when ordered in bulk quantities for business, educational, or sales promotional use. For information please write Special Sales Department, Hamilton & Cole Publishers, Inc., P.O. Box 104, 1520 Sawgrass Village, Ponte Vedra, FL 32082.

Cover designed by Peg Munsey

Library of Congress Cataloging-in-Publication Data

Pratt, Barbara V.,
    Own the Forest, Delegate the Trees: A Guide to Project Leadership/
    Barbara V. Pratt

ISBN: 978-0-615-19007-5
1. Leadership 2. Organizational Change 3. Strategic Planning 4. Project Management

To Dave

Thank you for the time to explore new possibilities, for being there through the rocky parts, and for celebrating the successes along the way. You make things so fun; 20 years with you is not nearly enough.

TABLE OF CONTENTS

Section I: Getting Started *1*
    Chapter 1: What's Here for You 3
    Introduction 3
        Why Bother? 5
        A Gap in Perception 6
        There is a Bigger Picture 8
        How to Use This Book 9

Section II: Create Effective Teams *13*
    Chapter 2: Understand Your Incoming Team Members 15
        Sponsors 16
        Business People 19
        Technical People 21
        Matrixed Staff 23

    Chapter 3: Project Organization Strategies 27
        Tier Concept 28
        Sample Project Organization Structure 29
        Projects Versus Programs 30
        Sample Program Organization Structure 32

    Chapter 4: Work Effectively with "Driver" Roles 35
        Governance 36
        Program Management Office 38
        Project Sponsor 40
        Program Manager 43
        Advisory Board 43
        Stakeholders 45
        Stakeholders: Resources 46
        Stakeholders: Operations Processes 48
        Consultants 49

    Chapter 5: Work Effectively with "Doer" Roles 53
        Project Manager 54
        A Special Message for Technical PMs 56
        Subject Matter Experts 58
        Business Analysts 63
        Technical Lead Analysts 67
        Identify Your "Right Hand" 69
        Business Process Implementers 71
        Developers/Programmer Analysts 72

Chapter 6: High-Voltage Resource Planning 75
    Sufficiency 77
    Strategic Sufficiency Session..77
    Team Member Time Allocation 81
    Using Mastermind Teams 85

Section III: Essential Start-Up Success Strategies *89*

Chapter 7: Time-Tested Structure and Routine 91
    Communicate Defined Roles and Responsibilities 92
    Project Schedule...94
    Project Plan 95
    Make Your Structure Successful 99
    A Final Word about Structure 101

Chapter 8: Master Your Due Dates 103
    Treat Your Given Due Date as Set in Stone..................................103
    Play within Due-Date Boundaries 105
    Create Compelling Alternatives..106

Chapter 9: Get in the Game of Negotiations 109
    Put on Your Business Hat..109
    The Negotiation Briefing...111
    Briefing Content 113
    The Back-and-Forth of Negotiations 115

Section IV: Resolve Common Challenges *119*

Overview 121

Chapter 10: Activate the Issue Resolution Process 123
    The Basics 123
    The (At Least) Weekly Meeting..125
    Format 126
    Facilitate the Agenda 127
    The Issues Log...128
    Sample Issues Log 129

Chapter 11: Know Corporate Politics, Culture, and Priorities 131
    Politics 132
    Culture 134
    Priorities..136

Chapter 12: Manage Resistance..139
    The What and Who of Resistance 141
    What Can You Do?..142
    Resistance to Change within Your Team 146

Table of Contents iii

Chapter 13: Pay Attention to People and Personalities 149
    People...150
    Personalities 154
    Tips for Working with Each Personality Type 156
    Your Personal Leadership 157

Chapter 14: Be a Compelling Communicator 161
    You are the Communications Hub 162
    Faulty Communications is the Root of Most Problems..............164
    Project Communications Basics 166
    Sharing Problems 167
    Your Personal Development..169

Chapter 15: Believe Solutions Are Possible.................................173

Chapter 16: Track and Resolve Resource Constraints 179
    Losing a Key Resource 180
    Needing New Resources or New Skills.......................................183
    Replacing a Key Resource...184

Chapter 17: Manage Due-Date Pressure 187
    Use Your Project Plan 187
    Demonstrate Your Commitment...189

Section V: Your Toolkit 193

Chapter 18: Tools & Logistics 195
    Project Briefings 196
    Project Plan (High Level) 198
    Project Schedule..199
    Project Organization Chart 200
    Project Roles and Responsibilities...201
    Detailed Project Plans 202
    Rolling Agenda 203
    Issue & Action Logs 204
    Meeting Calendar..205
    Problem-Solving Process 206
    Facilitation Techniques..207
    Master Contact List 207
    Meeting Minutes 209
    Status Reports 210
    War Room 213
    Email 215
    Voicemail 217
    Administrative Assistance and Delegation 217
    PowerPoint 219
    PM Gold! Tip Booklet 220
    Some Closing Thoughts on Tools 221

Section VI: Your 9-Step PM Checklist..223

    Overview..225
        Introducing the Nine Steps 225
        Step 1: Clarify Deliverables and Targeted Results 227
        Step 2: Plan Analytical Phase 230
        Step 3: Obtain and Launch Analytical Resources 233
        Step 4: Drive Viable Solution Alternatives..235
        Step 5: Prepare and Negotiate Alternative Implementation Plans 238
        Step 6: Obtain and Launch Implementation Resources 241
        Step 7: Manage Business Process and Technical Systems Design............244
        Step 8: Manage Development and Testing Activities...............................248
        Step 9: Manage Implementation and Evaluation 251
        Checklist Conclusion 253

Section VII: Incredibly Motivating Conclusion 255

Final Words..257

ACKNOWLEDGEMENTS

While this is a business book about project leadership; it is also a personal book sharing how I think, feel and act as a project leader. Many talented and caring people helped bring this book to life, including:

Amber Grady – I can't imagine a better personal and professional partner. You've helped make this entrepreneurial road an adventure!

My team of incredible book reviewers – Amy D'Angelo, Dale Beaman, Art Becker, David Cochrane, Tim Cole, Susan Cole, Elizabeth Copley, Richard Cordell, Kimberly Friedman, John Glowacki, Rich Grady, Karen Gutmann, Gwyn Myers, David Pratt, John Pratt, Charlie Raeburn, Diana Skiba, Erin S. Smith, and Michael B. Vavreck. Thank you for your powerful feedback; the wisdom, guidance and insight you provided were key to helping this book stay focused and real.

Kimberly Friedman, Michaela Miller, Steve Sadler, Rhonda Dunn, Lora Davis-Henningsen, Trish Michaels, Dawn LeMasters, Laura Kutz, Lizanne Bomhard, Ryan Schmelz, Gayle Wein, Phil Wein, Petra Boucher, Chris Igwe, Ann Elliot, Tron Hill, Scott Walker, Bradley Dugdale, Donald Mitchell, Vic Johnson – special people who have gifted me with their time and talent over the years.

Susan Snyder, Steve Vago, Sharon Crowell, Ted Adams, Mary Lynn Podolak, Dottie VonDette, Laurie Johnson, Lorena Coo – some of my earliest and still-best examples of project leadership in action.

Jack Canfield, Therese Quinn, Mark Victor Hansen, Jim Rohn, Loral Langemeier, Bob Proctor, Robert G. Allen, Nancy Altman, Ross Quinn, Tom Antion - for over 20 years you have been influencing my life by influencing my thinking and my way of looking at things.

To all the people who have worked with me on my projects over the years – Great people make great projects. You have been an integral part of my success. Thank you for the experience you've shared, the lessons you've taught me, and the fun we've had together.

Section I: Getting Started

CHAPTER ONE

WHAT'S HERE FOR YOU

INTRODUCTION

Project Leadership is not an administrative function. It's not a methodology. It's not a toolkit.

Project leadership is an active and interactive undertaking that involves strategy, tactics, relationships, and a keen desire to win. It is a Big Picture venture that requires vision, finesse, quick thinking, and advanced interpersonal skills.

If you are a project manager and you are not seeing project leadership in this way, then you have probably been playing a much smaller game than you, your team, and your company need you to play. No matter how hard or long you work, it will be difficult to succeed if you are only seeing a piece of the picture.

To succeed, the answer is to step up to the Big Picture: Own the Forest, Delegate the Trees.

4   Own the Forest, Delegate the Trees

Own the Forest, Delegate the Trees

The *forest* you own is your project. Owning the forest means you are in charge of the whole thing—the expectations of your internal and external customers, getting and keeping the right resources, the day-to-day progress of your team and their tasks, and the proactive communication and resolution of things that come up along the way that threaten your project's success.

The *trees* are all the individual components and aspects of your project: the people you report to; the people who report into you; the other resources you need; the things happening outside your project that might impact your project; your budget; your methods, tools and processes; and the business need and objectives which are the focus of all the rest.

The trees of a project can also be the minutia of project administration, the lure of crises, the intrigue of problem-solving, or the drama of human relationships and corporate politics. These things that come up to threaten your project can pull your eye off the business need and tempt you to stay among the trees.

When you switch your focus from the forest to the trees, you immediately limit yourself to what is directly in front of your eyes. From within the trees you can't see the overall health of the forest—how well you are meeting the business need. If you can't see it, you can't be in control of it.

When you own the forest, you are aware of all these things and you address them, but you don't get down and stay down in the trees. Instead, you gather enough information so you can make decisions to protect the forest, and then you delegate the corrective action and go back to focusing on the forest.

You can do this only if you lift yourself out of your project, and see it and lead it from above. When you own the forest – own your *project* – you accept full accountability for everything that is needed and everything that impacts the ability of you and your team to meet the business need on time, in budget, achieving targeted results.

This whole book was written to enable you to fully understand and put into action the 'own the forest, delegate the trees' concept. It shows you what project ownership looks and acts like on a practical, day to day basis. It tells you what and when to delegate. It shows you how to see, think, and act as a successful world-class project leader.

WHY BOTHER?

Lack of project leadership skills has been an issue in every company I've worked with. In my experience, many project managers (PMs) struggle as leaders. The PMs I have observed who struggle the most are the ones who share these fundamental misunderstandings:

- They're confused about what their companies really want of them and unaware of how having that understanding would empower them to do the job right.
- They underestimate the unique leadership challenges they face and the impact of being in an isolated, lonely position with an extraordinary amount of responsibility.
- They don't understand that their people skills are more important than their technical skills.

The answer to these problems does not lie within any tool or methodology. The things that keep PMs up at night usually have to do with people, conversations, briefings, decisions, and relationships. Your ease and effectiveness in dealing with these things are the direct result of the vision and leadership strategies you carry into your project.

This book, *Own the Forest, Delegate the Trees,*
- Lays out a real-life Big Picture of project management, and
- Gives you proven, effective leadership strategies, techniques, and action items for success.

This is not rocket science. Some of it may be quite familiar to you. Years of experience, both extremely successful and, in earlier times, less successful, have convinced me that this is THE make-or-break leadership information PMs must know. Here it is for you, condensed and collected into a single place.

Even if you are clear on these things and already a master project manager, realize the people around you may not be so clear. There is value in here for all key members of your team. You can share this book with people on your team and in your company to help them better understand your project and their participation in it.

A GAP IN PERCEPTION

Completion of the project is not what your company wants or cares about. What your company wants is for you to achieve a specific business goal. That seems pretty obvious, and you probably know it. But, the reality is that I see very few project managers—or project Sponsors, for that matter—whose actions show they understand this.

I conducted a survey[1] of both project managers and project management executives, and a very interesting pattern emerged. Within the project manager group, 85% felt comfortable they knew their jobs and were performing them well. On the other hand, the executives—across the board—said PMs in general performed poorly.

On a scale from 1 to 4, 1 being poor and 4 being excellent, all executives interviewed rated PMs as 1 or 2. In other words, **all ratings were below average to really poor**. Their written comments showed that these different executives individually arrived at the same conclusion: 5% of PMs are world class; 90% are average (and remember, their 'average' is a '1' or '2' ranking, which means 'performs poorly'), and 5% are really bad.

---

[1] The survey included 75 respondents from 31 Fortune 500 companies across seven industry segments.

What's Here For You

Given these statistics, you don't want to be "average" because the average PM is not delivering. If you are in that average 90%, your company will likely see you as underperforming.

Admittedly, this was a small survey. However, while you're thinking about these rankings, also consider these (summarized) Gartner[2] 2004 statistics on projects: The average project takes twice as long, costs twice as much, and delivers about 74% of its intended value. Gartner data indicates 85% of projects across the world are delivered late, over-budget, and with less-than-targeted results. In 1998, The Standish Group[3] reported essentially the same data and conclusions.

Obviously, when the statistics are this bad, there are more factors in play than the skills of the PM. These statistics also illustrate problems in how many companies address and handle change, e.g. slow decision-making, lack of accountability, missing-in-action Sponsors, unrealistic due dates, a blaming culture, and so on.

However, there are world-class PMs who deliver excellent results in the face of these challenges. After years of trial and error, education and mentoring, and on-the-job, often self-taught, training, I became one of them. I have been privileged to witness and work with other world-class PMs.

In *Own the Forest, Delegate the Trees,* I share with you the things master PMs know; things learned over time, sometimes at great cost—lessons that you can apply to become one of that much-in-demand top five percent.

---

[2] In their own words, Gartner is "the world's leading Information Technology research and advisory company." Project management is one of Gartner's core research areas.

[3] The Standish Group is a firm that, among other things, conducts primary research on project management and IT-related topics.

THERE IS A BIGGER PICTURE

It's my mission to free the human spirit in the workplace; to inspire people to give more to themselves, each other, and their company. While PMs may not be able to influence their company's culture as a whole, they absolutely do influence the day-to-day working life of all the people on their teams.

> "When the first Superman movie came out, [I would often say that] a hero is someone who commits a courageous action without first considering the consequences ... Now my definition is completely different. I think a hero is an ordinary individual who finds strength to persevere ... in spite of overwhelming obstacles."
>
> Christopher Reeve, Actor

You never thought of yourself as a hero? While that may be a bit of a stretch, there is no doubt that PMs are absolutely vital to a company's success.

PMs are the leaders of change. Without change, there is no progress. Without progress, there is no growth. Without growth, eventually, there is no company.

It's one thing for a company to have ideas for change and decide to implement them. It's the PM who takes those ideas and decisions and *makes the desired change happen*. If its projects are not unfolding successfully, the company is not unfolding successfully.

Of course, the PM doesn't do it alone. Effective PMs channel the massive talent, energy, creativity, and drive of many people to bring the desired change to life. When done well, projects can be beacons of change whose success ripples through and uplifts the entire organization.

HOW TO USE THIS BOOK

Before we go into any detail as to *how* the PM creates this impact and success, let's drop down to basics and get clear on four key terms and definitions that are used throughout this book:

1. What is a Project?
A Project is any initiative that has the following characteristics:
- Is temporary—it has a beginning and an end,
- Has a target, such that once the target is met, the project is no longer needed, and
- Requires the coordinated work of more than one person.

2. What is Project Management?
Project Management refers to the specific sub-set of business management functions that are required to launch, conduct, and then implement any project.

3. What is Project Leadership?
Project Leadership refers to the super-set of leadership essentials that are required to engage people and guide them successfully to goal achievement, while timely dealing with and/or maneuvering around the many obstacles and challenges that crop up along the way.

Executives assume project leadership is a part of project management. World-class project managers assume the same. This book teaches world-class project management; *whenever you see the term 'project management' from now on, it will refer to the combination of both 'project management' and 'project leadership' into one integrated approach.*

4. What is a Project Manager?

A Project Manager (PM) is a person who both manages and leads projects, from initiation through implementation.[4] The PM is accountable for delivering the targeted project goals, on time, on budget, and with the desired level of quality.

Now that we're clear on terms, here's a high-level look at what's in this book, and how you can navigate within it to get what you need.

This book is written as though you are a PM who is managing a large project. The lessons included in here can also be applied to small- and medium-size projects; I focused on the large ones since they require the broadest and deepest project management skills and knowledge.

The following chart shows the three broad responsibilities of a project manager, which are to:

a) Create, engage, and manage an effective team,

b) Lead that team to execute required work activities, and

c) Avoid, prevent, and/or resolve whatever issues and barriers come up along the way.

This entire book describes these responsibilities, along with the corresponding leadership strategies and actions you will need to take in order to execute these responsibilities with excellence.

---

[4] Ideally, the project manager will also provide post-implementation and rollout support to help the organization be able to handle the implemented changes. In many cases though, the PM is moved over to lead other projects instead. For specific PM roles and responsibilities, see chapters 4 and 5.

What's Here For You

Project Management	
Manage Project Lifecycle	**Resolve Ongoing Challenges**
1. Clarify deliverables and targeted results 2. Plan analytical phase 3. Obtain and launch analytical resources 4. Drive viable solution alternatives 5. Prepare and negotiate alternative implementation plans 6. Obtain and launch implementation resources 7. Manage business process and technical systems design 8. Manage development and testing activities 9. Manage implementation and evaluation	**Constant Crisis** • Issue Resolution Process **Environmental Barriers** • Corporate politics, culture, and priorities • Resistance to change **Relationship Glitches** • People and personalities • Communication pitfalls **Persistent Problems** • Solution complexity • Resource constraints • Due date pressure

(Left side vertical label: Create, Engage and Manage Your Team)

Each broad responsibility in the chart is covered in depth as follows:

- *Section I*: Getting Started – This section tells you what this book is about and how to find what you need. The 'Bigger Picture' segment also gives you an executive description of the world-class PM.

- *Section II*: Create Effective Teams – How to create, engage, and manage an effective team. This section covers project roles and responsibilities in relation to you as the PM. It also describes how to plan and obtain your team.

- *Section III*: Essential Start-Up Success Strategies – This section shows you how to successfully deal with three challenges you'll face at the start of each project: how to instill an appropriate amount of structure into your team's processes, how to handle due date expectations, and how to negotiate for whatever you need.

- *Section IV*: Resolve Common Challenges – This section addresses all the items in the 'Resolve Ongoing Challenges' column of the chart. Each issue is covered by an entire chapter that looks at the issue from both an executive and tactical perspective, and then gives you solution options.

- *Section V*: Your Toolkit – This section provides a list and description of practical, useful, and re-usable project management tools, with samples for most.
- *Section VI*: Your 9-Step PM Checklist – This checklist can serve you as either an introduction or a refresher of the basic activities of the PM throughout the life of a project. I placed this section at the end of this book, so it will be easy to find when you need it as a quick reference. It addresses the items in the 'Manage Project Lifecycle' column of the chart. The work is broken out into nine different steps, based on my own experience, with how the work tends to cluster itself.
- *Section VII*: Incredibly Motivating Conclusion.

This book will help you become a world-class project manager: more effective, more efficient, and a world-class business leader.

I have been a project manager for over twenty years, leading business teams and technical teams, working both inside corporations and as an external consultant to corporations. I've experienced most if not all of the same challenges, obstacles, frustration, and confusion as you.

Because I have walked in your PM shoes for a very long time, I know this about you: If you are voluntarily in the PM role, you are a person who, to a very strong degree, enjoys the challenges and obstacles you face. It's part of the fun for you.

But, for all of us, there are times when the challenges become overwhelming, and the possibility of failure—to meet the deadline, to deliver the results, to operate within budget, to have the team working effectively and productively together, to please the Sponsor or client—wakes us up in the middle of the night.

In this book, you will learn how to rise to these challenges and overcome them.

Let's get started ...

Section II: Create Effective Teams

CHAPTER TWO

UNDERSTAND YOUR INCOMING TEAM MEMBERS

In the next few chapters, I will describe generic project organization structures and typical project roles and responsibilities. In this chapter, you will see a more specific profile of the *person* stepping into your project.

The goal here is to help you put yourself in each person's shoes. Once you do this, you can tailor your communications to connect better with your team. This will help you start your project relationships on the right foot.

People operate at the height of their abilities when they are clear on what's expected of them, and when they feel understood and appreciated.

Your job as PM is to provide what your people need, so they can do their jobs well. Having an up-front understanding of just where people are likely to be coming from can help you do your job.

Typically:
- Business people don't see how big their role needs to be,
- Technical people don't see the boundaries of their roles,

- Sponsors prefer to be disengaged, and
- Matrixed[5] staff and their line managers will tend to start strong and then gradually disengage from the project over time.

These are some pretty gross generalizations, I know. In fact, this whole chapter is full of gross generalizations. Nonetheless, these generalizations play out so consistently across projects and companies, I feel comfortable giving them to you as guidelines. Guidelines like these can help you put yourself in other people's shoes more quickly, so you can figure out how best to bring them on board. Listen to people carefully and be ready to adapt to those people who do *not* fall into these generalizations.

Note: *The section that follows contains references to various project roles and terms with which you may or may not be familiar. Many of these are defined within this section; the rest are defined in Chapters 4 and 5.*

SPONSORS

Depending on the nature of your project, the project Sponsor could come from either the Information Technology (IT) division or some other business division.

The assumption of the Sponsor can vary widely from person to person. Still, the generalization I feel very safe in making to you is this: The Sponsor prefers to be far less engaged than you need him or her to be.

In some cases, the Sponsor is assigned as a figurehead role, meaning they are given the Sponsor title in the project without the backing of a time commitment. In many cases, the Sponsor expects to spend little more than an hour or two a week on your project.

---

[5] Matrixed people are borrowed people, lent to projects for a specified period of time to perform a specific body of work. They have other "real" (line) managers with hire and fire authority. Matrixed people report to project managers for this project-related work.

Understand Your Incoming Team Members

Likely assumptions of the Sponsor:
- As the PM, you'll be doing it all.
- The Sponsor's role is to collect status reports from you; your responsibility is to make sure the status is "good."
- On rare occasions, you may bring an issue to the Sponsor, in a beautifully wrapped PowerPoint package, to forward to other executives to get a decision about the project.

The truths of the matter are:
- As the PM, you are dependent on the Sponsor to help you sell the company on the true resource needs and the right due date and scope of the project.
- The Sponsor will be meeting in person with you anywhere from two to eight hours a week to review the project status and engage in resolving any potential show-stopping issues that come up.
- Your communications with your Sponsor will largely be informal and ideally face-to-face.
- The Sponsor has routine communications accountabilities to senior executives about the progress and issues of your project. The Sponsor is the face of your project within the company, and to external consultants and vendors.
- The level of Sponsor engagement directly impacts the level of your credibility and authority as PM. When people know you are backed by the power and influence of your Sponsor, they'll give you more of what you need, and give it to you faster.

In order to effectively engage your Sponsor, you must:
- Make sure you have the right Sponsor. This may feel out of your control, but the truth is, it's usually a pretty simple thing to identify the person in your company who is best positioned to be your project's Sponsor. Often this involves a delegation from a figurehead Sponsor to an active Sponsor. This usually works very well. Maybe the new person will carry a different title, such as Business Program

Manager. Just make sure you get someone with the power and influence you need, who will step up to the time commitment.[6]

- Make sure you have the right project organization structure around your Sponsor, such as the Advisory Board, Governance bodies, and Key Stakeholders. You need people above and around your Sponsor who will be holding the Sponsor accountable for project results and who will team with your Sponsor as needed to close pivotal issues and decisions. *(Chapters 3 thru 5 cover designing the full project or program team.)*

- Take your Sponsor to breakfast and to lunch, and drop by their office with coffee from time to time. Let them know you expect to be part of their lives for the duration, that you are on their side, and that you are on top of things.

- *Be on top of things!* The best thing you can do to create the necessary relationship with your Sponsor is to be superlative in your role to them.

- Think about their needs, what they need to know, and what they need to report to their superiors.

- Keep it simple; they don't need to know all you know about the project. Speak and write in bullets.

- Rise to their level and pay attention when they give you feedback. For example, if your Sponsor says, "I couldn't read all you sent; what's the bottom line?," then next time, just give the bottom line.

- Respect your Sponsor's time. Think before you walk into his or her office, before you pick up the phone, before you send an e-mail.

- No surprises! The more you can protect your Sponsor from getting egg on the face in some meeting with superiors, the more your Sponsor will trust and respect you.

- Meet your commitments. You expect others to honor their commitments, so you must honor yours. Set the bar high for everyone, and be sure to meet it yourself.

---

[6] If I see my Sponsor cannot fulfill their role for whatever reason, I work directly with them to identify and get a commitment for their delegate. First, I lay out—in excruciating, painful detail—the role, responsibilities, and weekly time commitment my project needs from the Sponsor. This is usually enough to get the Sponsor's concurrence that we need a delegate. Then we discuss who *could* perform the role well (it is usually someone who is a direct report of the Sponsor), and what we need to do to free that person's time, so they can work on the project. The Sponsor most often justifies this resource need with their executive and assigns the work to that delegate.

Understand Your Incoming Team Members

I can't say I do all of these things, all of the time, on all of my projects. However, I can say I do all of these things, *most* of the time, on all of my projects. Without a doubt, doing these things has been a key factor in my own project success.

It IS extra work on your part to do this degree of thinking, pre-planning, and communications. Most PMs don't do it; they either haven't considered it, or they don't see the value of it. Many of you reading this, even if you agree, won't do these things because it takes an extra couple of hours a week. Nevertheless, I guarantee it is part of what it takes to achieve success at the world-class level.

And, it is absolutely worth it. When you treat your Sponsor like this, you are showing respect. Your Sponsor will recognize pretty quickly that you are smart, competent, strategic, and business-savvy and will appreciate you putting yourself in Sponsor shoes, so you can provide support with excellence. Once these things are seen, your input will be trusted and your recommendations given full weight. Your Sponsor will be more willing to go to bat for you and your team. In the long haul, you will be saving yourself far more time, work, and stress than you may imagine.

BUSINESS PEOPLE

Business People are typically found in these project roles: Sponsor, Governance, Advisory Board, Stakeholders, Business Analysts, and Business Subject Matter Experts.

In many corporations, PMs come from the IT division. When this happens, people outside of IT often think of the entire project as being a "technical" project, and they assume the bulk of the work will be done by "technical" people. This assumption is often untrue, especially for larger projects and programs.

So, the assumptions of the Business People on your team are likely to be:
- Your role (the project management role) is big.
- Their role is small.
- You are lucky to have them.

Own the Forest, Delegate the Trees

Now the truths of the matter are these:
- Your role is even bigger than they think.
- Their role is also bigger than they think.
- You ARE lucky to have them (assuming you've successfully negotiated for the active participation of the right people, per Chapter 6 *"High-Voltage Resource Planning."*)

I recommend you *act as though* these three items are truths at the start of each project, and make it your routine to immediately and respectfully educate your team members on their roles. Even when people do have a good understanding of their roles at the start, it can't hurt to clarify. If you take the time to let people know your expectations of their assigned project roles, you will increase your chance of success exponentially.

Remember, some of these people have never worked on project teams before. Some have worked on poor project teams. Some people have worked on successful project teams before, but they are in new roles now. Many or most of the people may be working with you for the first time; perhaps you have different expectations of them than their last PM did.

Don't assume business people know what you need and expect from them. Don't assume they understand and have agreed to the amount of time you need from them. Do assume it's your responsibility to make these things clear to them as part of your team and to nail down their individual time commitments.[7] Be prepared to get re-commitments from these people two or three more times, especially at the start of each major new phase of the project. There are always new things coming up in their business area that will tend to pull these people away from your project. You need to keep reminding people that your project needs them.

---

[7] You need a documented resource plan, to use both in managing your resources and in communicating your resource needs and timing requirements. Your company may require that you use a specific resource planning and tracking tool, such as Microsoft Office Project or SAP. I use a simple Excel spreadsheet format, which you can view at www.ProjectLeadershipGold.com.

Understand Your Incoming Team Members

TECHNICAL PEOPLE

Technical People are typically found in these project roles: Developers/Programmer Analysts, Technical Lead Analysts, Technical Subject Matter Experts, and IT Governance.

It's my experience that most projects suffer from a lack of needed business resources. When this happens, the technical people on the project will usually try to pick up the slack. Over time, technical people have become used to not getting needed business support. Often they stop expecting it and stop asking for it.

When this happens (even though projects are beginning to get more executive attention and the possibility of getting needed business resources is more likely), many technical people keep wearing the hat that says "I must do it all." This assumption is often untrue, especially for larger projects and programs.

Still, at this point in time, the assumptions of the Technical People on your team are likely to be:

- Business people will not participate as needed.
- We must pick up the slack.
- We are great at this "saving the day" stuff; we'll pull this off or die trying.

Now the truths of the matter are these:

- IT people are NOT great at saving the day. When an IT person or team picks up business tasks as well as their own, it usually means they still miss the deadline and/or results targets. For them, it's an over-and-above-the-call-of-duty win. *But for the project, it's a miss, not a success.* Remember from the Introduction, 85% of PMs think they're doing great work, yet 85% of projects across the world are delivered late, over-budget, with less-than-targeted results.
  Companies don't acknowledge or reward individual feats of heroism in projects. A late project is a late project no matter who dies trying to save the day.

- The Project Manager is responsible for negotiating and managing a *viable* project resource mix and timeline so the technical people will not have to pick up a business resource slack. IT people have plenty on their plate already.

I can hear PMs the world over saying, "Hey! I TRY to get the business resources I need, but my Sponsor (or company) won't give them to me!"

Here's the thing: As the PM, you are the leader of your project team and the owner of your project plan. No one else. Once you say "Yes" to whatever resources and timeline are given to you, understand you are making a personal commitment to your Sponsor, your company, yourself, and your team that you WILL deliver.

If you believe you cannot deliver, then you *must* negotiate the project scope, the resources, and/or the timeline. If you fail in those negotiations and do not believe you can deliver to expectations, *then don't say "Yes."* It's unfair to everyone involved. Instead, bring your negotiations as high in the organization as you need to go, following the appropriate chain of command. Remember, you have the clearest view into your project. If you see something that is impossible, then it's your responsibility to communicate that effectively to decision-makers. (*Chapters 8 and 9 provide much more detail and guidance about the content and conduct of these negotiations.*)

It is my observation that most projects fail to receive needed resources or fail to establish achievable due dates because the Project Manager did not effectively prepare and present the business case[8] that would persuade decision-makers.

So, to lead your technical people, let them know you expect the business members of the team to participate as planned. Let them see you hold the business members to that standard. Then, keep an eye on your technical people because they can tend to over-commit themselves from habit. Make sure you and your leads check on all interim deliverables to see if anything is

---

[8] By "business case" I am not referring to the full, formal business justification of the project. I mean the more limited cost-benefit analysis that is performed when the team creates solution alternatives and recommends one of those for management approval.

Understand Your Incoming Team Members

falling behind. Question all IT-provided due dates carefully to ensure they pass the "reasonableness" test and that they allow at least a 15% to 30% fudge factor for all the unknowns.

One of the reasons I love IT people is because they usually say, "Yes I can!" when the rubber meets the road. One of the reasons it can be challenging to manage IT people is because they'll say, "Yes I can!" even when they can't. They need your help to keep their expectations of themselves realistic.

MATRIXED STAFF

Matrixed people are typically found in these project roles: Business Analysts, Technical Lead Analysts, Business Subject Matter Experts, Technical Subject Matter Experts, Business Process Implementers, Developers, and Programmers.

In other words, most of your hands-on working resources will likely be matrixed to you. In effect, you are borrowing them for your project. This means they will have line managers other than you. These "real" line managers are the ones responsible for their performance reviews, their salary reviews, and ultimately their future in the company.

So, the thinking process of the Matrixed Staff on your team likely goes something like this:

- It is better for me to please my line manager than my project manager, so
- I will work on the project as much as I can, but
- If my line manager tasks me with too much, then I'll do less work on the project, so I can meet the priorities of my real boss.

The truth of the matter is:

- They're exactly right, *unless*
- You insert yourself and your project into their performance and salary/bonus review process, and

- You monitor each matrixed person's time and progress on a continual basis, and work with the assigned individual, then his or her line manager if needed, should their time or progress start to slip.

It is very important that you understand, accept, and work within the boss-employee cultural relationship that exists in your company. Most are established as a dependent relationship: Employees are dependent on their bosses for annual performance reviews. In these reviews, their bosses tell them their worth to the company, expressed in raises and promotions.

In a matrix situation, you have a person working for you—full- or part-time—who is still 100% dependent on a different line manager for salary increases and promotions. You need to step in and reach an agreement with these line managers, to make sure you get a proportionate share of input to both.

You want to do this for pretty obvious reasons. Unless your matrixed team members see that you, too, have influence over their money and promotion possibilities, their first loyalty will always be to their line managers. If they are allocated to your project 50% of the time, that means they remain allocated to their line managers 50% of the time. If their line managers ask them for more than 50% of their time, then what influence do you have to entice them to say "no" to their line managers and honor the full 50% due you and your project?

Matrixed people are in a tough position. They frequently and repeatedly are in situations where they need to make a tough call: "Where do I spend my time?" Common sense says one of their guidelines will be "What's in it for me?" As the PM, it's your responsibility to give them good, valid reasons for giving you the full negotiated time allocation. Get firm agreements with their line managers about how much input you'll have over their performance and salary reviews. Get it in writing.[9] Then communicate it clearly, in person and in writing, to your matrixed people.

---

[9] A sample of a written agreement between a PM and a line manager is on our website.

Understand Your Incoming Team Members

This is a big deal in terms of importance. It is not that big a deal in terms of time and action on your part. No matter what size your team, most of your matrixed resources will report into a much smaller number of line managers. These line managers will very often be Stakeholders in your project, so you will be meeting and talking with them anyway.

Most line managers will welcome anyone helping them in any way to write these performance reviews! I recommend that you make a broad proposal to all line managers, such as "For any person matrixed to me on a 20% to 25% basis or more, I get proportionate input to both performance and salary or bonus reviews."

You will need to follow through on this commitment when the project is complete and/or it is annual performance appraisal time. When appropriate, collect input from your team members. In a large project, you may delegate this performance assessment work to the people who worked most closely with the matrixed person.

This whole "input to their review" concept is not new. Paying this much attention to it is. The more clarity you get on this topic between you and the line managers, and between you and your matrixed people, the better for you and your project. It underlines their time commitment to you. It shows you expect to get the full resource allocation you've been awarded. It lets them know they'll be hearing from you if you start receiving anything less.

By the way, people *like* to know these things. They like to know where the lines are drawn, and whether the lines are dotted (representing a temporary, matrixed reporting relationship) or solid (representing a direct, ongoing reporting relationship). They like to know what time commitment you need from them. This information helps them be in control of how they manage their time across their priorities.

CHAPTER THREE

PROJECT ORGANIZATION STRATEGIES

The purpose of this chapter, and the next two Roles and Responsibilities chapters, is to:

- Help you, the PM, understand each role,
- Help you understand the options and opportunities you have in building a great team, and
- Help each player understand their role in the project, and all the other roles.

The size, complexity, and scope of your project work dictates whether you are managing a project or managing a program. Repeating from Chapter 1, a *project* is a temporary initiative, launched to achieve a specific goal, requiring the coordinated work of more than one person. A *program* is a collection of two or more projects that combine to achieve an integrated business goal. Roles and working relationships change a bit between projects and programs.

TIER CONCEPT

Before we look at sample organization charts, let's first take a look at the general shape of a project's organization. All projects have a basic egg timer, or hourglass, shape that looks like this:

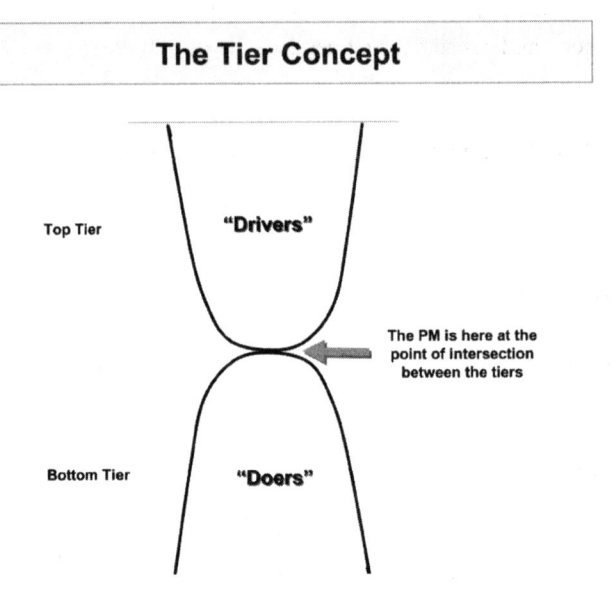

The Tier Concept

Top Tier — "Drivers"

The PM is here at the point of intersection between the tiers

Bottom Tier — "Doers"

The Tier Concept is the idea that some people function mainly as Drivers on your project, and others function mainly as Doers. Drivers set direction; they allocate resources, and they make pivotal decisions. Organizationally, people who do these functions—regardless of their job title in the company—are in the top tier, the Driver Tier, of your project.

Other people are Doers. They actively plan, manage, design, test, and implement all the work tasks of the project. Organizationally, people who do these functions—regardless of their job title in the company—are in the bottom tier, the Doer Tier, of your project.

While you are not the *only* connection point between these two tiers, you are the one responsible for the effective communications and working partnership between them.

SAMPLE PROJECT ORGANIZATION STRUCTURE

A simple project organization chart places a Sponsor plus a few other key influencers in your Driver tier, and it places you, two team leads—one business, one technical—plus a pool of Subject Matter Experts, implementers, and consultants (if needed) in your Doer tier.

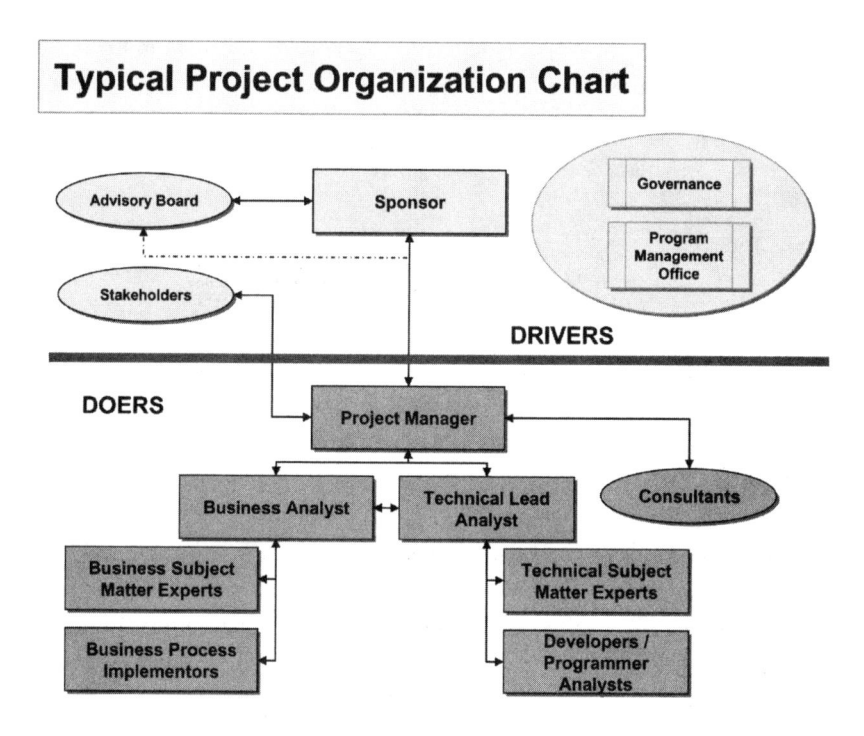

Typical Project Organization Chart

DRIVERS
- Advisory Board
- Sponsor
- Stakeholders
- Governance
- Program Management Office

DOERS
- Project Manager
- Business Analyst
- Technical Lead Analyst
- Consultants
- Business Subject Matter Experts
- Technical Subject Matter Experts
- Business Process Implementors
- Developers / Programmer Analysts

You may or may not use consultants on a project. If you do, you are most likely to use them as contract labor to add hands and 'been there, done that' knowledge and experience to your Doer tier. In this case, you would assign your consultants to the appropriate roles in that tier.

For projects, your time and focus as a PM is, *very* roughly, split about 20% to 25% towards the Driver tier and 75% to 80% towards the Doer tier. As the PM, you are in the Doer tier, as the bulk of your time is spent planning, leading, tasking, and managing all the other Doers.

PROJECT VERSUS PROGRAMS

There is no hard and fast rule for defining the point at which an initiative is clearly a program, not a project.

Managing a program versus managing a project calls for the same basic work activities, but the tactical focus and the balance of your time and attention will shift. The larger and more complex the initiative, the further to the right you will move along this continuum:

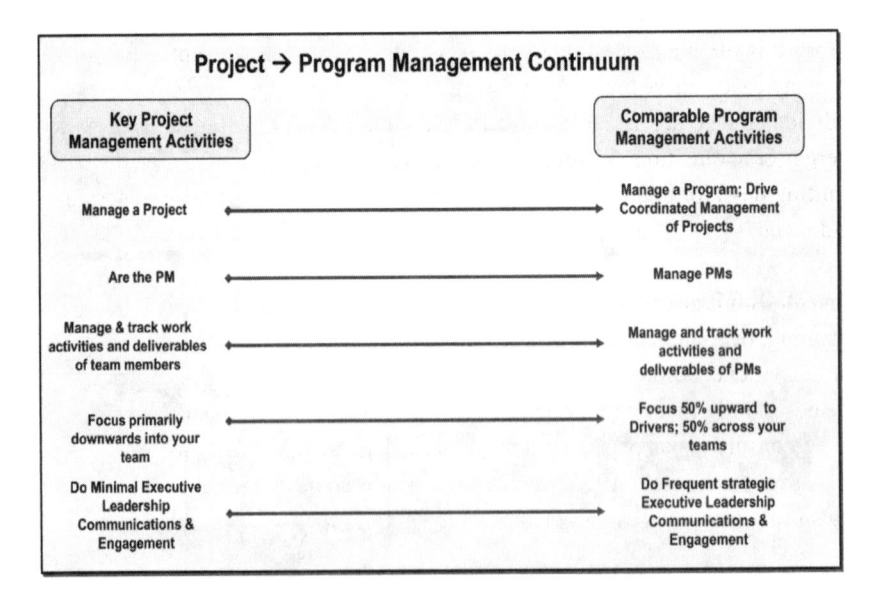

Project → Program Management Continuum

Key Project Management Activities	Comparable Program Management Activities
Manage a Project	Manage a Program; Drive Coordinated Management of Projects
Are the PM	Manage PMs
Manage & track work activities and deliverables of team members	Manage and track work activities and deliverables of PMs
Focus primarily downwards into your team	Focus 50% upward to Drivers; 50% across your teams
Do Minimal Executive Leadership Communications & Engagement	Do Frequent strategic Executive Leadership Communications & Engagement

In designing the right structure for your project or program, think about how to tactically manage the work. By this I mean, how many PMs do you really need to get the job done?

A key thing I play with in designing my teams is figuring out how much project management I can and should delegate to others on my team. If the work is significant, I go for true, experienced PMs who already know project management methodology basics. If the work is fairly small, I look at the people in my analytical roles to see if they demonstrate some of the key management and leadership skills I need. I design my team structure starting with either the generic project or program organizational framework provided in this chapter, and then I customize it by taking into account the actual skills and talents of the people I can put in the key roles.

If you do not understand the work effort enough to figure this out, then you may need executive consulting help. When you are given a huge, complex effort, it is often a task neither you nor your company has attempted before. In many cases, these are one-time-only efforts for both the company and the individuals who are asked to do them. Examples of such initiatives include a merger or acquisition, outsourcing, downsizing, launch of a new product, shutting down or opening up a new division, business process reengineering, and so on.

Enormous initiatives like these often call for new analysis, thinking, and planning, over and above the basics of project management. You may need to buy experienced brains to either do or help you do these new things, in order to successfully meet your company's needs. For this type of work, you are using consultants as peers, advisors, and management hands ... not necessarily as contracting resources. You might also need additional consulting resources as contractors to do some of the actual work.

32   **Own the Forest, Delegate the Trees**

SAMPLE PROGRAM ORGANIZATION STRUCTURE

With the above considerations in mind, let's take a look at one possible *program* organization:

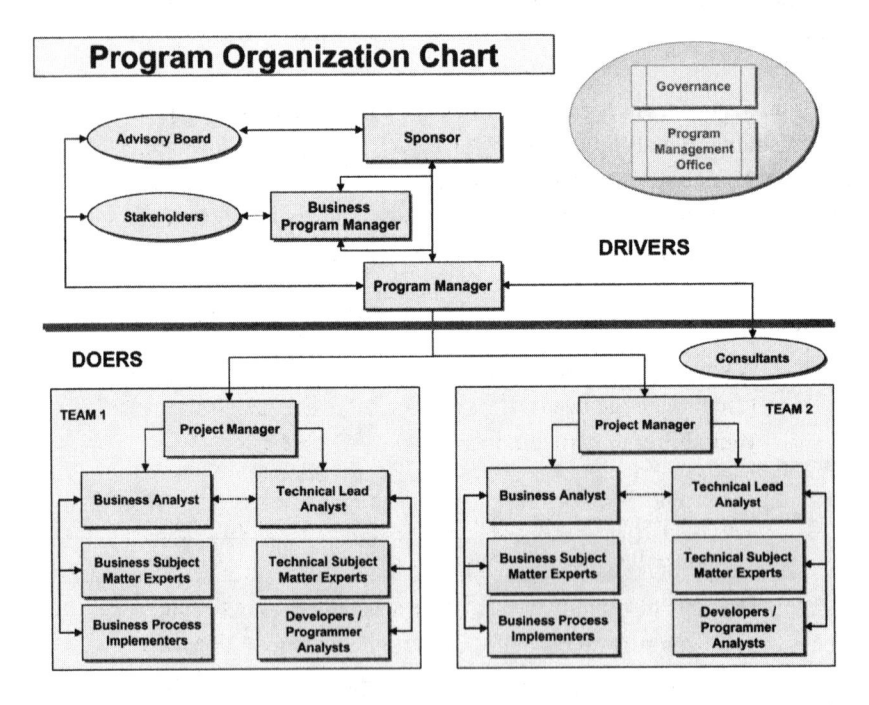

Program Organization Chart

- Advisory Board
- Sponsor
- Stakeholders
- Business Program Manager
- Governance
- Program Management Office
- Program Manager

DRIVERS

DOERS   Consultants

TEAM 1
- Project Manager
- Business Analyst
- Technical Lead Analyst
- Business Subject Matter Experts
- Technical Subject Matter Experts
- Business Process Implementers
- Developers / Programmer Analysts

TEAM 2
- Project Manager
- Business Analyst
- Technical Lead Analyst
- Business Subject Matter Experts
- Technical Subject Matter Experts
- Business Process Implementers
- Developers / Programmer Analysts

In a program organization, the sheer quantity of people adds enormous weight to both the Driver and Doer tiers. Note that **as the Program Manager, you are actually out of the Doer tier and into the Driver tier.** Your time shifts dramatically to about 50/50 between the two tiers.

This is a critical role change that many PMs miss when they start managing programs versus projects. When you lead a program, your work shifts dramatically as 50% of your time is spent understanding, communicating, negotiating, and guiding all the other Drivers. You gather progress, status, and issue information from the Doer tier and synthesize, summarize, and communicate it at the program level. To the other Drivers, you represent their primary point person into the whole program.

Project Organization Strategies

With the remaining 50% of your time, you are functioning as a Driver for the PMs who report into you. As the program manager, you drive the work of your PMs. You ensure they have clear and documented project objectives, plans, schedules, meeting and communication structures, issue resolution processes, and so on in place. You make sure the objectives, plans, schedules, and work activities of each project blend together appropriately so nothing gets missed and all elements of the program are delivered on time and in budget.

Program management is an active and accountable function, not just administrative. The PMs report to you as their manager for their work in the program. You are responsible for managing these PMs as they execute the project management of their slice of your overall program. You retain full responsibility for the results of the entire program.

Summary

- A key early challenge in each project is to design and staff the right team, given the needs of your project, the available resources, and your ability to barter and negotiate to adjust the availability of resources.
- Use sample project organization charts as a starting place, and then customize them to suit your project needs and circumstance.
- Pay special attention to clarifying which roles and people belong in your Driver tier versus your Doer tier. Generally speaking,
    - You lead, manage, and drive the work and results of the people in the Doer tier, and
    - You are guided, directed, and given resources and key decisions by people in the Driver tier.
- As your projects get bigger and more complex, you need to adjust the amount of time and focus you give to your various responsibilities and activities. You will need to consider delegating some tactical project management work to others, in order to free more of your time to see, manage, and coordinate across the entire work spectrum.

In the next two Roles and Responsibilities chapters, you'll see which roles have the most flexibility. These are the roles you can most easily tweak to mix and match real people, with their unique strengths and weaknesses, to the specific functional needs of your project.

CHAPTER FOUR

WORK EFFECTIVELY WITH "DRIVER" ROLES

In the last chapter, you reviewed a project and a program organization chart, and read about the Driver and Doer tiers. In this chapter, we will use the more comprehensive *program* organization chart as the basis, and focus on Driver roles and responsibilities.

You will see a typical profile of the person stepping into each Driver role and get recommendations for how you can start your relationships with these Drivers on the right foot.

For each role, you will see its primary responsibilities, plus one or more strategies and tips you can employ to create an effective relationship with the people in that role.

36 Own the Forest, Delegate the Trees

Remember, people operate at the peak of their abilities when they are clear on what's expected of them and they feel understood and appreciated.

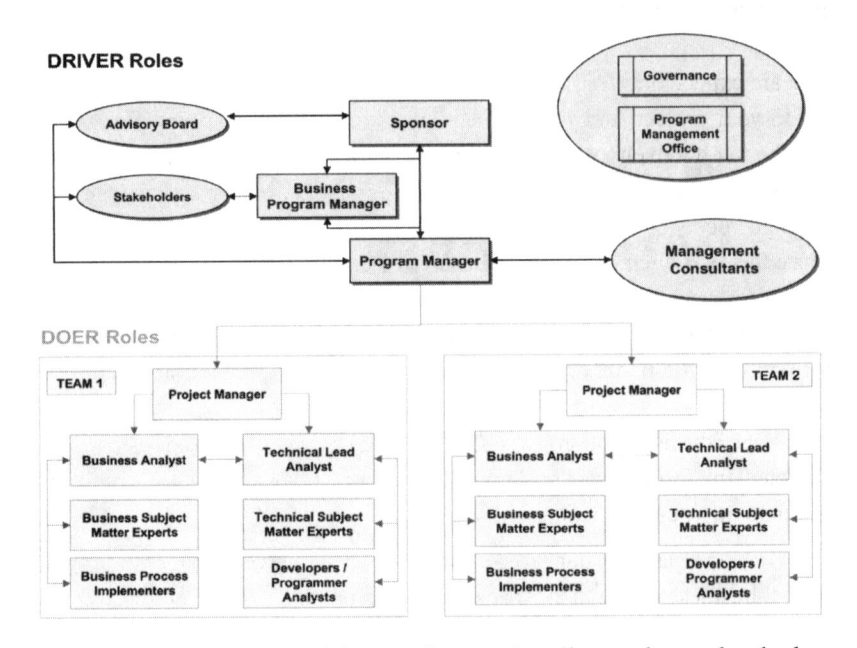

DRIVER Roles

```
Advisory Board ──┐
                 ├──→ Sponsor            Governance
Stakeholders ────┤         │             Program Management Office
                 │         ↓
                 └──→ Business Program Manager
                           │
                           ↓
                     Program Manager ←──→ Management Consultants
```

DOER Roles

TEAM 1 — Project Manager
- Business Analyst ↔ Technical Lead Analyst
- Business Subject Matter Experts ↔ Technical Subject Matter Experts
- Business Process Implementers ↔ Developers / Programmer Analysts

TEAM 2 — Project Manager
- Business Analyst ↔ Technical Lead Analyst
- Business Subject Matter Experts ↔ Technical Subject Matter Experts
- Business Process Implementers ↔ Developers / Programmer Analysts

The focus in this chapter and the next is not primarily on what each role does, though I do define that. The focus here is on *what you as the project manager need to do* in order to effectively manage the people in these roles.

There is a quick-reference, short Project Roles and Responsibilities bulleted chart available on our website: *www.ProjectLeadershipGold.com*.

GOVERNANCE

Project Governance refers to the decision-making processes, policies, and procedures that a company follows to make decisions about which discretionary projects to fund and staff.

As the PM, you will not be interacting much with the Governance Board. Usually, the only time you'll be dealing with the board is in the decision phase when your company is trying to figure out whether they'll be doing the

Work Effectively with "Driver" Roles

project at all. Companies vary a LOT in the level of involvement they expect from you in this phase. It ranges from zero input all the way to the expectation that you will lead the decision justification effort.

If you are expected to lead the decision justification effort, then that effort itself IS your project, and you'd manage it like any other. Your targeted result would be to effectively provide sufficient data, information, and a recommendation to enable company decision-makers to make an excellent "go/no go" decision about your project. The deliverable you would create to capture this particular collection of information is usually referred to as either the business case, or the decision package. A second deliverable is often a related executive briefing. Typically, the Project Sponsor will present this information to the Board. You may be invited to address any questions.

In this book, the assumption is the Governance process has already been completed, the project is a "go," and you have just been assigned to lead it. In this situation, your interaction with the Board is two-fold:

1. At the start of your project, read or review the Governance-approved business case and any backup documents that justify your project. These lay out the measurable results your company intends your project to achieve. This information, coupled with any nuances added by your Sponsor and other Stakeholders, tells you what your team must deliver in order to be successful.

2. Lead or participate in ongoing project reporting processes that collect and summarize project progress and results information for the Governance Board, who will verify that delivered projects are achieving the expected results as laid out in the business case. The bigger and more costly the project, the more frequent and extensive this type of reporting will need to be.

PROGRAM MANAGEMENT OFFICE

A Program Management Office (PMO) is an organizational entity that exists in many companies. The people in that organizational unit provide a variety of support functions to your project that could include:

- Program management – the company's program managers may reside in the PMO
- Project management expertise – PM mentoring and coaching services
- PM training and certification services
- Project management software, tools, and methodologies – research of best practices; selection, implementation, and training of PM support systems
- Portfolio management & administration – collection, analysis, reporting, and executive reporting of cross-enterprise project status, resource, and budget data
- Project quality assurance – monitoring and measuring of project progress and success
- Project intervention – support for PMs in getting off-track projects back on track
- Project plan administration and status reporting – provision of processes, systems, and templates for formal, consistent project reporting
- Personnel time and expense administration and reporting – provision of processes, systems, and templates for project time and expense tracking and measurement
- Related methods and standards such as Sarbanes-Oxley, CMM (Capability Maturity Model), and so on, which you may be required to integrate into your project

Work Effectively with "Driver" Roles

Your company may or may not have a PMO. If it does, then you'll need to be familiar with any project requirements and guidelines your PMO may offer and/or mandate. Know what is required versus what is recommended. Decide which recommendations make sense for your project. Identify any requirements that could threaten the success of your project, assemble your logical arguments, and then identify and meet with an authorized PMO decision-maker and negotiate any exceptions to their requirements.

Per SEI (Carnegie Mellon Software Engineering Institute): *"You must use professional judgment to interpret [required] practices... practices must be interpreted using an in-depth knowledge of the model being used, the organization, the business environment, and the specific circumstances involved."*

Sometimes the most successful strategy for your project is to quietly bypass a generic process or procedural requirement that you deem harmful to your project. This is a call you will need to make from time to time. There tends to be a handful of people in most large companies who appear to value form over content, to the exclusion of common sense. To openly engage with them can take boatloads of your time and energy.

Talk to your leads and talk to your Sponsor. If you get agreement from these people that, for this project, it makes sense to ignore a particular requirement, and it's the kind of requirement that is pretty low key and invisible, and you all agree it would probably take more time than it would be worth to openly lobby for an exception, then make the strategic leadership decision to "just ignore it."

Don't make these decisions lightly. In most cases, the value the PMO and other such groups offer you and your project is good, and it is to your benefit to follow their guidelines and methods. Nonetheless, you are accountable for meeting the business needs. You are accountable for meeting the due dates. You are accountable for the hundreds of daily decisions that either keep your project on track or move your project off track. So, with careful consideration of any risks, do what you must to position your project for the highest likelihood of success.

PROJECT SPONSOR

Sponsor responsibilities are to:
- Provide mission and direction.
- Serve as 'champion' for the project, selling its benefits to the organization to increase awareness and enthusiasm, while mitigating resistance to the upcoming changes.
- Be the final decision-maker (excepting for those major projects that require, for strategic decisions, a governance decision).
- Provide, or ensure provision of, high-level project requirements, objectives, vision, and results measures.
- Review proposed and delivered processes and confirm that requirements are met.
- Ensure provision of resources.
- Give final approval of program deliverables and controls.
- Be the business escalation point for critical issues.
- Participate in program executive communications as needed.
- Meet with you routinely (at least weekly).
- Keep on top of the project status, and the issues you bring to his or her attention.
- Keep you informed of any changes occurring within or outside the company that may impact your project.

If you think all sponsors are going to do all, or even most, of these things well and of their own volition, then you may be in for a big surprise. Your project Sponsor can make or break your project. Here's the deal: It's up to you to make sure they make it. Many PMs don't see it this way, and so the Sponsor often becomes the failure point in a project.

In my projects, I've always taken the position that I am leading this project *for my company*. This is the *Own the Forest, Delegate the Trees* mindset. Ultimately, I'm accountable to the company. My company has assigned me a specific person to report to in the chain of command: my Sponsor. That person may or may not have a clue as to what I need and expect of them.

Work Effectively with "Driver" Roles

In my experience, most Sponsors don't have a clue. It's not because they're clueless, or not interested, or not capable, or even too overworked. It's usually because they have a preconceived idea of what a Sponsor does,[10] and they go about executing to that idea. Usually this idea is wrong, and it came about because the last PM(s) the Sponsor worked with never established the parameters for the right relationship.

You have to realize this: You own the project. Even though the company holds the Sponsor accountable, and even though the Sponsor's compensation may also be tied to the project's success, on the most _tactical_ level, you are the driver, the leader, and the manager of this initiative.

Although you report to them, sponsors typically need you to clearly outline and explain what you need from them and why. You must communicate the time commitment and the specific activities you need from them. You know your project. You know the project lifecycle. You know how vital the Sponsor's active and ongoing engagement is to the success of the project. It's a mistake to assume your Sponsor knows all these things, too.

Instead, assume two things:
1. They are overloaded with a million other responsibilities.
2. They don't know what being a good Sponsor entails.

Once you understand this, you will see it's up to you to let the Sponsor know how to engage effectively. And if they can't—most likely due to time constraints—then they need to go with you to help you get another Sponsor assigned or to free themselves from other work, so they can devote enough time to this project.

---

[10] As a refresher, here are the likely Sponsor assumptions from Chapter 2: a) As the PM, you'll be doing it all; b) The Sponsor's role is to collect status reports from you; your responsibility is to make sure the status is "good;" and c) On rare occasions, you may bring an issue to the Sponsor, in a beautifully wrapped PowerPoint package, to forward to other executives to get a decision about the project.

Your company expects you, the PM, to know how to run a successful project—not your Sponsor. Even if your Sponsor has done the job before, remember that statistically most projects are overdue, over budget, and deliver underwhelming business results. Chances are that any Sponsor role played before was not a very effective one.

Not only must you ensure that your Sponsor understands what you need, but you must also make the need compelling enough that your Sponsor's boss and company executives understand what the Sponsor must be available to do. The goal is to get your Sponsor released from some other activities, so your project gets the time, attention, and priority it requires.

So: In order to help your Sponsor support you, you need to first support them.

> *"Help me help YOU!"*
> Tom Cruise to Cuba Gooding Jr., in the movie *Jerry Maguire*

By the way, in most large projects, Sponsors will designate a point person for you to work with on a day-to-day basis. This point person is often the most-impacted Stakeholder. (*Briefly, a Stakeholder is a person whose business area is impacted by the project. See the Stakeholders section later in this chapter for a clearer definition.*) The Sponsor retains the responsibilities above, but daily project and resource decisions and issues are delegated to this point person.

There is confusion as to what to call this 'point-person' role. I've seen that person called the Sponsor, the Program Manager, the PMO, the Business Director, and so on. I'll call them the Business Program Manager (BPM) in this book.

BPMs are your daily counterpart on the business side of things. They support you in getting Stakeholders to give you resources. They work within the business community to both get the project work accomplished and to prepare the business community to handle the resulting new processes. You clear key issues and decisions together. They are a 'business clearing house' to you; you are a 'project clearing house' to them.

Work Effectively with "Driver" Roles

To close this section on your Sponsor: You are responsible for your project's success. You can only achieve that if your Sponsor is engaged and effective. Make sure you consistently prepare them well and support them well in the things you expect them to do for you and your projects.

PROGRAM MANAGER

This title can mean different things. In this book, I use the title Program Manager to indicate someone who manages a program, which is a collection of individual but tightly related projects that combine to achieve a specific business objective. The success of each *project* is needed in order for the *program* to be successful. This use of the term Program Manager is the most common. If you are a Program Manager by this definition, everything in this book on *project* management still applies to you; the scale will just be different.

ADVISORY BOARD

The Advisory Board is a crucial group of people. They are the executives who have influence over the direction and success of your initiative. They may be recognized as an advisory board, but very often they are simply the handful of executives with enough power that if they sneeze, your project may come tumbling down.

The role of the Advisory Board is to:
- Be the executive representative for their business area, to the project.
- Provide input, advice, and counsel to the Sponsor.
- Give input, direction, and executive requirements to you.
- Communicate the priority and importance of the project to their business area.
- Allocate representative stakeholders to the project.

You want to establish a connection with these people in the first week or two of your project; I schedule one-on-one meetings to do this. You need to let each member of the Advisory Board know that you know who they are, that you acknowledge their importance to the success of your project, and most importantly, you need to personally collect and/or confirm their desires and expectations of your project. You are responsible for fulfilling those needs and expectations; make sure you both have the same understanding.

You may do this with your Sponsor. It's often very helpful to have you and your Sponsor hear the same thing from each key executive, and it's a good relationship builder all around. The executives see that you care about their needs. The Sponsor observes you functioning on his or her side, hears you ask intelligent questions, watches you establish rapport with each executive, and sees you accept joint responsibility for the outcome.

I usually make a point of casually connecting with the executives again, one-on-one, within a few days of this three-way meeting. I don't *schedule* this one-on-one, because I don't want to waste their time, and I don't want to do anything formal without my Sponsor. I have this second meeting for three reasons: to help the executives remember me in case I need to come to them for a later decision, to show them I remember *them* and I care about their input, and to give them the opportunity to share any additional thoughts with me.

It usually works like this: I check the executives' calendars so I know when they'll be leaving their offices for meetings or for lunch, then I drop myself nearby, one by one, and engineer casual meetings in the hallway. In these meetings, I greet them, walk with them a few steps, and remind them we spoke a few days ago about XYZ project. I ask if there's anything they've thought of that they want to tell me or they think I should know. Often, they'll start communicating valuable information to me even before I've asked the question because they *have* had additional thoughts they've wanted to share.

Work Effectively with "Driver" Roles

I almost always get new information at this point and a keener insight into what they really care about. They might emphasize a point already made, or clue me into a political or personal relationship situation I'll need to keep an eye on. This is great stuff! I immediately let my Sponsor know each time I "run into" someone like this and what I was told... except in the rare circumstances where the Advisor shares negative information with me about my Sponsor.

I don't share personal negative feedback I receive about my Sponsor. I simply use it to help me understand when and how I can best engage my Sponsor in certain escalation activities and negotiations. For example, if I'm told by the CFO (Chief Financial Officer) that the CFO thinks my Sponsor is incompetent, I might spend more time preparing my Sponsor for any needed meeting with that CFO, and/or I'll work with that CFO directly, and/or I'll suggest my Sponsor take their boss with them when they meet with the CFO. In other words, I'll do what I can to support my Sponsor within the political and relationship realities parameters I'm given.

STAKEHOLDERS

Lots of people and managers will be impacted by your project. Few of them will be named Stakeholders for your project.

Stakeholders are managers[11]

- Whose business or technical units will be significantly impacted by the progress and results of your project
- Who have been given the right to give you input, and to be kept abreast of project plans and progress
- Who are responsible for preparing their business or technical areas for the impacts that result from the project

---

[11] They could also be functional representatives in staff positions, such as Corporate Counsel or an internal auditor.

Stakeholders are generally at a lower management level than Advisors. In large projects, Stakeholders will often directly report to Advisory Board members. For example, the Senior Vice-President (SVP) of New Products could be an Advisor, and the Manager of New Products could be a Stakeholder. Where the Advisor gives you input, direction, and high-level requirements, Stakeholders give you people resources, and they work within their business area to prepare it for the implementation of your project.

Most often, Stakeholders have two 'stakes' in your project:
1. **Resources** – their people are matrixed to you to perform project work, and
2. **Processes** – the operational processes Stakeholders manage will change once your project is implemented.

Your role with Stakeholders is to enable them to get benefits from the resource and process stakes they have invested in your project.

STAKEHOLDERS: RESOURCES

Stakeholders need to know exactly which of their people you'll have working on the project, how much time you need, and for how long. Stakeholders are often the key 'line managers' who are matrixing their people to you. Whenever they give you a resource, it creates a void within their own organizations that must be addressed. Most often, it means some other activity needs to stop or get backfilled, so your project can be started.

Your responsibilities in getting the resources you need from Stakeholders are to clearly state your project's resource needs, get the Stakeholder's personal agreement, and receive and effectively use those resources.

Expect Stakeholders to probe your resource requests. The more resources they give you, the more resource gaps they need to close on their end. You may need to engage the related Advisor, and/or the Sponsor, to help Stakeholders free resources for you. They may need authorization to stop certain other activities.

Work Effectively with "Driver" Roles 47

Do all this FAST. The work of your project can't start until you have people. If you have a 12-week project and it takes two weeks for you to request resources and for a Stakeholder to assess their options, find solutions, transition current work activities from the person you requested to someone else in their organization ... then your project is 1/6 over already.

The following list contains factors that will increase your ability to get the resources you need from Stakeholders:

- *High Priority* – If your project is a very high priority, it will trump the other things the desired people are working on, and you will be able to get them taken off other things, so they can work on your project.

- *High Impact* – If your project will have a very high impact on that particular business area, even if the project itself is not that high, you will also be able to get the people you need. You may need to lay this story out to your Sponsor and the desired persons' line managers, so they see it. Your persuasive argument is: Since this project is going to significantly change how your area works, it is in your best interests to give us your best people to help ensure this project does it right.

- *High Influence* – If you have an executive who is passionate about this project, then they can assist you in convincing others to give you resources for the higher good.

- *Great Relationship* with the Line Manager – In the absence of these other items, if you personally have a great relationship with desired resources' managers, you may be able to persuade them to give you the resources you need just because you support each other.

- *Compelling Risk Case* – If you can quantify the cost to the project of NOT getting the particular people resources you need, then that cost/benefit analysis could persuade Stakeholders to meet your request.

STAKEHOLDERS: OPERATIONS PROCESSES

Stakeholders need as much advance notice as possible about the specific changes to their business operations that your project will make. Will jobs need to change? Will new skills be needed? Will reports be different? Will screens be different? Will their customers be seeing or hearing anything different? Do customer scripts need to change?

While you are busy implementing change, Stakeholders are busy getting their business areas ready to operationally work with those implemented changes. Business staffing may need to increase or decrease. Training may be needed. New job skills may be needed. Manual processes may now be automated. Inter- and intra-departmental routines may need to change.

Your responsibility to Stakeholders is to give them timely information about your project's status and activities. Most of this will be done routinely to Stakeholders as a group.

When Stakeholders have a LOT to do to get their units ready for the changes coming from your project, you will need to provide them more help. Large change usually means a large project, which usually means your Sponsor already designated a Business Program Manager (*this is the Sponsor point person described in the Sponsor section above*). That is the ideal person who will work closely with Stakeholders on a frequent basis. If there is no BPM, then the alternates to work closely with Stakeholders are you, your Business Analyst(s), and/or your Sponsor. [*See the "Business Analyst" section within Chapter 5 for more information about how projects work with impacted business areas to prepare them for changes resulting from the project.*]

> *By this point, you are already getting a good idea of the Own the Forest, Delegate the Trees mindset. If you would like to actually experience this mindset in relation to your own projects, and practice these tools and techniques hands-on, you can do this within our training workshops. For more information see our 'Professional Services' and our 'Solutions' pages within our website: www.ProjectLeadershipGold.com*

Work Effectively with "Driver" Roles

CONSULTANTS

You can find a Consultant to do almost anything for you on your projects. Typically, you will bring consultants on board to:

- Provide experienced advice and counsel to you when you're tackling new territory in your projects, e.g. outsourcing, merging, dramatic process change, etc.
- Provide experienced key leads and managers when your projects are large and you must delegate project management work, and you have no available internal experts
- Provide hands-on business and IT technicians as extra resources to do the work

Sometimes a consultant or consulting firm will be assigned to work with you by the Sponsor or senior executives.

I have been lucky to have worked with consultants on many of my projects. In my early, smaller projects, I would generally bring on consulting *technicians*. I brought them on board because they gave me more hands, and they already had the specialized knowledge and expertise I needed. To keep our scope and meet our due date, the extra expense of hiring contractor-type consultants was worth it. When I use consultants for these purposes, I am using them as Doers, not as Drivers, within my project.

It wasn't until I started working with management and executive consultants that I began to see the value of using consultants as partners and mentors within the Driver tier. A typical U.S. corporate middle manager works in an average of one company in five years.[12] A typical management consultant has worked in at least five times as many companies.[13]

---

[12] The January 2004 Employee Tenure Report prepared by the Bureau of Labor Statistics notes that workers in management, professional, and related occupations had a median tenure of five years.

[13] Management consultancy services take approximately 12 months to complete, per ABS Business Consultancy, 2006 website figures.

When I bring a team of management consultants on board, I am buying a deep and rich experience base. They have done what I'm about to do, in other companies, several times before. They already know what works and what doesn't. They did their beta testing on someone else's dollar. They are already a team, with communication practices in place that make them strong and effective as a unit. They've got tools and methods already, which they'll share with me and my team.

Management Consultants bring a wealth of knowledge and experience that you as PM can learn and absorb. It will make you a better PM and leader; it will make you more valuable to your company and the market, and it will introduce you to new ideas and techniques that would never cross your path otherwise.

To work effectively with Consultants, you must make sure you:

- *Lay out your needs*, expectations, deliverables, due dates, roles and responsibilities, etcetera very clearly, and in writing.
- *Decide which method* and approach to use, when your consultant's methods are different from your own.
- *Establish interim deliverable reviews* and checkpoints, so you can ensure they are achieving the progress you require.
- *Give them access to you.* Since they are 'outsiders,' consultants will see and observe activities, patterns, and facts that you and your other team members will not. They will spot problems or potential problems that others will miss, giving you the chance to fix them while they're small.
- *Give them access to your team.* Look for opportunities to partner your expert consultants with your best internal people. This makes the project a great learning experience for your internal people, and it helps build the company's own skill base so external consultants are less needed the next time the company launches a similar project.

Work Effectively with "Driver" Roles

- *Make leading your consultants a high priority.* Consultants are generally powerhouses who will deliver more, faster. They can help you set the pace and structures of your project. You need to be ahead of them direction-wise, or you'll be paying top dollar for dead time and missing big opportunities.

Last, I recommend that when you hire management and executive consultants make a point of developing an intimate working relationship with them. Use them as your personal coach, mentor, and guide. Pick their brains. Debate best practices. Discuss alternative approaches, tools, and methods. Your company is paying a lot for what's in their heads; get as much of it as you can during the course of your project. Whenever possible, engage your core leads and team members as well, so they can also benefit.

CHAPTER FIVE

WORK EFFECTIVELY WITH "DOER" ROLES

In Chapter 3, you reviewed both a project and a program organization chart, and read about the Driver and Doer tiers. In Chapter 4, we covered the roles and responsibilities of the Driver tier. In this chapter, we will cover the roles and responsibilities of the Doer tier. I will use the *program* organization chart as the base.

You will see a typical profile of the person stepping into each role and get recommendations for how to help your relationships with Doers start off on the right foot.

54   **Own the Forest, Delegate the Trees**

```
                    Governance
    Advisory Board ← Sponsor    Program Management Office
    Stakeholders ← Business Program Manager
                    ↓
                Program Manager          DRIVER Roles

─────────────────────────────────────────────────────
DOER Roles                                  Consultants

TEAM 1                              TEAM 2
    Project Manager                     Project Manager
  Business Analyst ↔ Technical Lead    Business Analyst ↔ Technical Lead
                     Analyst                              Analyst
  Business Subject   Technical Subject Business Subject   Technical Subject
  Matter Experts     Matter Experts    Matter Experts     Matter Experts
  Business Process   Developers /      Business Process   Developers /
  Implementers       Programmer        Implementers       Programmer
                     Analysts                             Analysts
```

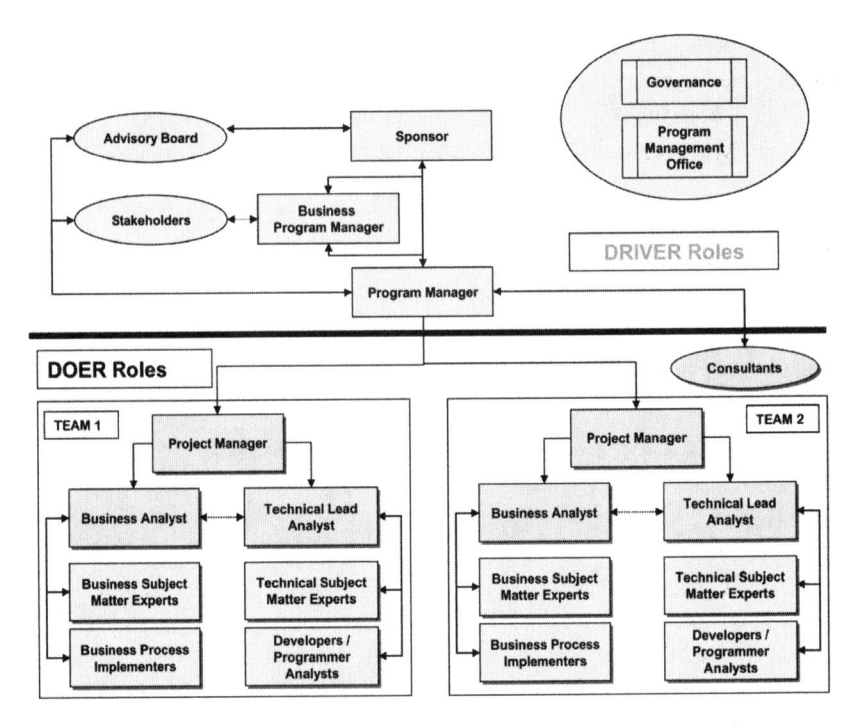

PROJECT MANAGER

Your primary duties as the Project Manager (PM) are to:

- Plan and manage the work from requirements definition through testing and implementation.
- Assign, manage, and coordinate Business Analysts, Leads, Subject Matter Experts (SMEs), Developers, and Process Implementers according to plans.
- Be accountable for implementation and rollout of processes according to plans.
- Resolve project issues that arise.

This entire book is for you, so I'm only going to add one thing here: Don't kid yourself into thinking this book is for everyone else.

Work Effectively with "Doer" Roles

From Chapter 1, you know the statistics: 85% of projects, on average, are implemented in twice the time, at twice the cost, and they deliver about half the desired benefits. You and I both know there are many factors besides our skills as PMs that are causing these poor results.

Nonetheless, the quality of our project management skills *is* a core factor that determines whether we are in the 15% success group or the 85% failure group. It's important that you understand how executives and project monitoring groups such as Gartner are measuring project success: If you miss a deadline, even though your company has moved the due date out to match your later delivery, you missed the deadline. You're in the 85%.

Most project managers I've met consider themselves in the top 15%, even when they're way past their due dates or way over budget. They give themselves an "A" for effort, and they say "I would have gotten the project in if it weren't for _(fill in the blank)_ " (my sponsor, the company culture, my project plan software, the fact that my team is in different time zones, the unfair due date, etc.). Their project is late, over budget, and under delivered; their company is disappointed with these results, yet these project managers still consider themselves to be successful.

You won't be able to resolve every issue, all of the time. But, the top 15% consider every one of those variables to be their responsibility. They don't point fingers and blame the variable; they take responsibility for it, and step up and take action. *They own the forest.*

It's important on many fronts that you, the PM, commit yourself from the very start to this: You are picking up full accountability for your project. Yes, visible accountability carries risk. Taking accountability also brings with it power and authority. Once you pick up accountability, you have a lot more leverage to do things right—which can actually reduce your risk.

A key to my success has been that I pick up the whole thing; I own it. People tend to be relieved when someone assumes clear leadership. As long as the leader is competent, people will follow.

Ownership of a project means taking full responsibility for the solution, its design, development, and implementation. Ownership includes doing all this in accordance with a mutually agreed upon plan, schedule, and resource mix.

Note that ownership does not mean <u>doing</u> all this work. It does mean making sure this work gets done by the people whose job it is to deliver those results and who have the best skills and talents to do them.

Project management is a game. The stakes are high and the pace is fast; that's what makes it exciting. YOU are the person who is making change happen. You are the implementer of your company's new direction. You are the leader of a team of forward-thinking people who are injecting new life into stagnant products, systems, and operations. When you succeed, everyone succeeds. Accept this full responsibility; go forth, and succeed.

A SPECIAL MESSAGE FOR TECHNICAL PMs

Technical PMs often have a problem drawing a clear line between their old role as technicians and their new role as PMs. It's important that you know which hat you are wearing at any given time.

What do I mean by "old role as technician"? If you are an IT technician, the kinds of activities you would do in a project would include things like coding, testing, performing systems design and analysis, brainstorming best technology tools and platforms, studying architecture models and requirements, participating in detailed technical solution sessions, and so on.

If you're not in IT, technical activities would include those things where you are providing your specialized business knowledge and expertise—for example knowledge of finance, accounting, operations, current processes, marketing, product development. Your technical expertise is your knowledge of how and why the business conducts its work each day.

These things are not project management. When you do them, you are not functioning as a PM; you are being a Subject Matter Expert (SME) on that particular technology.

I was lucky to have an insightful boss who warned me about the technician-to-PM transition when I first faced it. I had already successfully led a number of IT projects as the supervisor and lead technical expert when I asked to be the PM of a really exciting new project that was bubbling up. She asked me, "Barb, are you sure you really want this? If you take the project manager role, then you'll be doing mostly administrative work. You won't be able to do the technical stuff anymore, and I know you like that."

I said, "Yes, I want it!" (Frankly, I didn't quite know what I was getting into; it just looked like an interesting challenge.) But, the warning stuck with me, and I used it as my guideline to keep me focused on being the project manager, not the technical expert.

That focus made all the difference in the world.

I linked arm-in-arm with my business counterparts and stayed focused on strategy, planning, communications, structure, and clearing my team's path. The project ended up being a winner in every aspect for my company, and for everyone involved.

If you think of yourself as a technical or IT project manager, the best advice I can give you when facing a big project is to take your technical hat off and start thinking of yourself as a "business project manager." The difference is subtle, but it can help create a core shift in your perception of yourself, what you do, and how you relate to all your constituents.

Here's the bottom line: No project is approved unless somebody somewhere is convinced that the result of your project will yield a business benefit. That business benefit is the only reason your project was given its resources. Your PM role is to deliver that benefit.

When you think of yourself as a business project manager, you will keep your focus on delivering the expected business benefit of your project. That will be your ongoing motivator; that is the vision you will keep in front of your team and your constituents. It will be the focus of every conversation and communication you have about your project.

The primary difference between a technical Project Manager and a Business Project Manager is this: The technical PM will tend to focus on and speak about detailed technical activities and issues, whereas the business PM will tend to focus on and speak about an assessment of how key project, management, and resource *facts* and issues *relate to achieving targeted business benefits*. The focus on facts and business benefit is far more powerful and more likely to yield the results you want.

SUBJECT MATTER EXPERTS

Subject Matter Experts (SMEs) can be either business or technical experts. In either case, their primary responsibilities are to:

- Define or provide requirements for their areas of expertise.
- Review and approve interim and final process designs and deliverables.
- Participate in process and system testing as needed.

These are the people who know their business area. They know the processes, the players, the tools, the timing, the communications, and the interactions. While other team players know how to design and implement change, your SMEs are the ones who know how things are done now, and how they'd like them to be done as a result of your project.

For each business area that your project will, or may, touch, you want that area's best experts to work with you on your project. These people are easy to identify: They are the ones everyone always goes to for information about their area. If you ask, "Who is the best expert in this business area?" then you will keep hearing the same name(s). That is the SME you want.

Work Effectively with "Doer" Roles

Getting SME resources assigned and engaged is going to be one of your biggest resource challenges. The problem is, as the experts, everybody else wants them, too. They are leaders in the day-to-day operations of their area, and they are likely already involved in other projects. They are probably overbooked already, and now here you come. [*See the previous "Stakeholders" section for ideas to help you get the SME resources you need.*]

SMEs can be difficult to manage, because they are difficult to coordinate. The work of a SME is often ad-hoc: SMEs are interviewed for some information. That information gets analyzed, which raises more questions. So, SMEs are interviewed again. SMEs often need to be interviewed together with other SMEs when the team is trying to put together a picture of the whole system. SMEs themselves may not know all the answers to the questions they get asked by the team, so SMEs have to go find other people in their area, interview them, and then bring those findings back to the team.

The SME work I've been describing is very fluid. Questions lead to answers that lead to more questions. While this is the nature of all players within the analytic phase of your project, the special challenge with SMEs is that you usually get a much smaller percentage of their time. If I get 20% of a SME allocated to me, in theory, I get eight hours a week of their time.[14] However, I can't plan that time for them in advance—no one knows what questions our analysis will surface. What I really need is eight hours a week at the drop of a hat, with the possibility that in some weeks eight hours may grow to twelve hours and in other weeks eight hours may drop to six hours.

If you don't get this drop-of-the-hat flexible access, you will fail to meet your deadline. I'm not being dramatic here; lack of SME resources when you need them is a project killer.

This is your key PM challenge with SMEs, so let's dive in and play this out. I'll give you a narrative description and then a graphic description of what happens when key resources are not flexibly available:

---

[14] Twenty percent of a 40-hour workweek equals eight hours.

Say my company agrees to give me 20 SMEs, each at 20% allocation during my six-week analysis phase. This means I get 160 hours a week (20 SMEs times eight hours a week each), or 960 hours over the six-week period.

In Week 1, I have some formal, scheduled meetings set up to induct my 20 SMEs into my project. I give them material to read, and a heads-up of what my team will be asking them. All 20 of my SMEs attend these scheduled meetings. I get all 160 of my SME hours this week; 100% of what I need. My team leads immediately schedule some initial SME-specific meetings for Week 2.

In Week 2, 16 of my 20 SMEs attend their initial SME-specific meetings. In these meetings, new questions arise, so follow-up work and meetings get scheduled. But, four SMEs miss half their scheduled meetings in Week 2 because they had other commitments. Those missed project meetings get postponed into Week 3. So, in Week 2, I've lost 16 hours of SME time (four SMEs times half their planned eight hours each); I received 90% of my allocated 160 hours.

In Week 3, we're in full ad-hoc mode. Questions arise along the way, and SMEs get asked to meet on the fly. However, many SMEs are otherwise scheduled: John SME can't make a meeting on Tuesday, but he can make one on Thursday. Jane SME, who needs to be interviewed with John, can only meet on Wednesday. Both John and Jane are technically available to me for eight hours, but I need them together and I can't get them together this week. I've lost all eight hours for each of them, because when people miss meetings, they also miss the follow-up research and work that would have been assigned in the meetings. This situation happens also with Fred and Sam, Ethel and Pete, and Susan and Tina. Though they are all allocated, they are not flexibly available this week. Therefore, my project has lost eight hours times eight people in Week 3, or 64 hours; I received 60% of what I need.

Work Effectively with "Doer" Roles 61

The following chart illustrates this resource situation. If I am experiencing resource shortfalls on my project, I will put together a picture such as this to show my Sponsor, and I will lay out the facts behind it. The facts and pictures tell the story that helps my Sponsor understand why it is a serious issue that requires intervention:

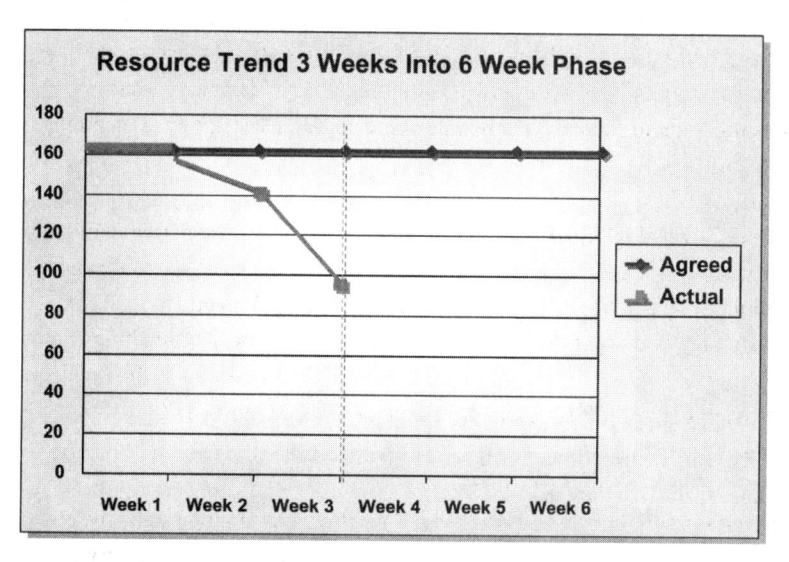

Resource Trend 3 Weeks Into 6 Week Phase

(Chart showing Agreed line flat at 160 across Weeks 1–6, and Actual line dropping from 160 at Week 1 to ~140 at Week 2 to ~96 at Week 3.)

"Sponsor Stan, I've got a situation here that needs your help. We asked for, and were allocated, 480 SME resource hours for this three-week period. However, we actually received only 400 hours, or 83%.

"The project is at the midpoint of the analysis phase, and here's what's been happening: I received 160 hours in Week 1, 144 hours in Week 2, and 96 hours in Week 3. When you add all this up, it means the project has experienced a 17% resource shortfall overall. If we continue to experience that average 17% shortfall, our six-week analytic phase will take *seven* weeks to complete. This is a one-week project delay.

"*But, the situation is even worse than that.* See how the trend is getting worse? Even though it *averages* to a 17% shortfall, this past week we had a 40% shortfall! If the situation continues to worsen as the trend suggests, then the one-week delay will become even longer. I need you to work with me to get Stakeholders to make this project a priority, to make sure their assigned people are available, and to help us reverse this trend, so we can get back on track."

This situation is a simplistic example. It doesn't reflect all the compromises teams make to try to accommodate people's various schedules. It does reflect that when people miss meetings, or postpone meetings, it measurably hurts the project schedule.

The point is, be on top of your ACTUAL resources. Allocated resources don't count. Actual, accessible resources count. You need to be right on top of all your SME resources, so you can point out instantly when a tiny miss or two is adding up to a project delay. Make sure your SMEs know if their lack of availability is causing problems. Make sure your leads track and report this information to you.

Then, make sure you contact your Sponsor and Stakeholders immediately if SME resources are not as available as you need them. They will probably need to work with your SME to clarify how they will support your project.

While this can be frustrating, and definitely time-consuming, if you can look at this objectively it all makes sense. The analytical phase is the first phase in your project. So, your Stakeholders (usually also the SMEs' line managers) and SMEs have just:
- learned about your project,
- heard they need to work with you,
- agreed to a certain resource allocation, and
- are working to give you that resource.

Usually, if a person is moving from one set of activities to another, they get time to wind down the first and start up the second. If that wind-down/start-up process takes three weeks, in most corporate situations then that would be good. However, it is not good enough in project situations because projects need to start up at warp speed. In a project situation like the one I described above, a similar three-week start-up period would create a measurable delay in the overall project timeline, which is *not* good.

Work Effectively with "Doer" Roles

You understand these dynamics. In most companies, most of the people around you do not yet understand these dynamics. You need to keep track, communicate, and educate people about your true resource needs, the actual resources you are receiving, and the company's cost if you are not getting what you need. Then you need to persuade people to either give you the resources you need, or accept delays in your project. Most of the time, people will find a way to provide what you need once they understand the context.

BUSINESS ANALYSTS

The primarily responsibilities of the Business Analyst (BA) include:
- Elicit and document business requirements.
- Confirm that technical analysts understand requirements.
- Develop test cases and test plans for business users to validate delivered systems and processes.
- Create process documents and job aids as needed.

On small to medium projects, your Business Analysts (BAs) will usually do straight business analysis work: They will elicit 'as is' business process information from SMEs; they will participate in 'to be' solution design; they will document business requirements; they will support developers during the technical design phase; they will construct business test plans and initiate any needed business training, and they will coordinate SMEs and others through the testing and training execution.

On large projects, when I need to delegate some project management responsibilities to my key leads, I look first to other PMs and then to Business Analysts as possible leads. As you see, the Business Analyst is a person who needs to be strong in analysis, communications, and management. A PM needs these same strengths. The inherent talent, personal characteristics, and interpersonal skill sets are the same; the main differences between the two are tools, methodologies, and experience.

Own the Forest, Delegate the Trees

It's pretty easy to teach a Business Analyst to pick up basic project management responsibilities. Just provide them with sample deliverables and an overview of the work you need them to do. Because they have very strong analytical skills, they are able to see how to tweak the samples to suit this project, and 'see' how to go about doing the work that the samples reveal.

On large projects, I generally try to create PM/BA pairs. On smaller projects, I am the PM who pairs with the BA(s). The PM brings project management knowledge and experience. The BA brings (collected) business process knowledge and experience, and a close connection to the SME and business operations aspects of the project.

The more you can get your PMs and BAs to be in sync on your project, the better. You get important cross-training; you get needed business/IT checks and balances, and you get the exponential value of their combined brainpower and experience applied to areas of mutual concern.

I'm going to go off on a tangent here for a few paragraphs. Bear with me, and I'll tie it all together for you at the end:

On large projects that involve both major IT activities AND major business activities, what often happens is that formal project management structure, tools, and planning are only used on the IT aspects, and informal processes continue to be used on the business operations aspects. You'll see a detailed Microsoft Project work plan for all IT-related activities, but the PM only sends routine status reports to the business Stakeholders who are accountable for discovering, designing, developing, testing, and implementing the business operational changes demanded by the project. These changes are largely 'out of scope' in most projects. They tend to be executed by business people informally, without following project standards and methods.

The role of preparing the business people to handle any technical or business process change tends to belong to the line managers of the impacted business areas. The project provides information to these line managers via the Stakeholder and Subject Matter Expert roles, but does not usually provide direct project management leadership, structure, tools, or methods.

Work Effectively with "Doer" Roles

As another gross generalization, here is a chart that shows a common split of project-related work that falls under the recognized project management umbrella versus project-related work that tends to fall under the operational line management umbrella. You can see that the full value your company wants from your project is only possible if all the things in this chart occur successfully:

Project Management	(Usually) Line Management*
Analyze existing business processes from a flow of information perspective, e.g. screens, reports, applications, data, information handoffs.	Analyze existing business processes from a business operations perspective, e.g. who does what, what skills are required, how much time is spent on what tasks (this work IS in scope when it's important to understand, so a best solution can be *designed*).
Design 'to be' processes including new screens, reports, applications, data, etc.	Design 'to be' jobs, organization, physical environment changes, training programs, new inter-unit communications practices.
Develop new screens, reports, applications, data, etc.	Develop new job descriptions, new org, new roles and responsibilities, new HR policies and procedures, new management and measurement practices and tools, new operating procedures.
Test systems, including business personnel working with new systems.	Practice new operating roles and procedures.
Implement, monitor, track, measure, evaluate system changes.	Implement, monitor, track, measure, evaluate business personnel and operational process changes.

* *If a project is designated as a Business Process Re-Engineering or Re-Design effort, then a lot more of these things will be recognized as in the Project Manager's scope.*

One of the keys to my success on large projects is that I bring much of this line management work 'in scope.' It just makes sense to me, so I include it. How can I deliver a successful business result if all I do is turn over an excellent IT system to hundreds or thousands of people who are in no way, shape, or form prepared to handle it?

The problems in picking this up lie in politics and fear. I remember the first time I really stepped up to the plate on this. I met with a pivotal line manager, and said, "We need to talk about how we'll be working together throughout this project." She looked me straight in the eye, totally serious, and said, "There's nothing to talk about. Here's how it will work: I'll tell you what to do, and you'll do it."

How do you partner your project management leadership skills, knowledge, and techniques with the actual leader of the business change, without stepping on their toes?

The answer is: Educate, communicate, explain, persuade, show, and lead by example. This all takes time, effort, and planning. This 'extra' work is something I delegate in part to my BAs to leverage their interactions with SMEs to include this extra dimension. (Notice how I've tied this all back to the BA role?) I also pick up this extra work myself by expanding my interactions with my Sponsor and Stakeholders.

The end result is that as people get clearer on the size of this informal, out-of-scope work, they recognize it needs more attention. Additional business resources are usually assigned. While the business operations activities are managed on a day-to-day basis by their line managers outside the official project umbrella, those line managers are supported by detailed information, recommendations, samples, methods, tools, and suggestions provided to them by the project's PM, BA, and SME resources.

TECHNICAL LEAD ANALYSTS

The primary responsibilities of the Technical Lead Analyst are to:
- Develop the high-level solution.
- Determine the technologies to be used—and not used.
- Design technical solutions to meet business requirements.
- Review technical solutions with the BA for approval.
- Communicate technical solutions to developers.
- Guide the detail technical solution design.
- Establish the method of integrating any new technologies into the current technology set.

Your Technical Lead Analyst is another key person on your team. This person is a senior IT technician, or manager of IT technicians. They have great analytical skills that they apply to the IT aspects of your project.

Similar to your BAs, your Technical Lead Analysts can often be delegated project management tasks and responsibilities. The thing to watch out for if you do this is their ability to communicate effectively. Some technical people have the ability to speak about technical things to a non-technical audience; other technical people simply can't or don't do this. If your Technical Lead can't cross that communications line and translate technical concepts, plans, issues, and solutions so business people can easily understand them, then restrict your Technical Lead's project management responsibilities to just the IT leg of your team.

As PM, a very important thing you need to do for your team is ensure the proper involvement of your technical people in all phases of your project. Your Technical Lead will usually be the first person you start this with. They will then be your point person to get—or prevent—involvement from the other IT people on your team.

In many companies, the tendency is to withhold IT involvement from those aspects of the project that require the most business input. The obvious reason is that these aspects need business input, not IT input, so IT attendance would be a waste of resources.

A less obvious reason IT involvement is withheld is the communications issue I mentioned before. If you have IT people who can't see and speak about their thoughts and ideas in business terms, then it is likely they will start speaking about technical concerns and constraints that aren't appropriate at that stage of the project. This can make those work sessions painfully ineffective.

But, if you don't have *some* IT leads in key early sessions where business people are describing how things currently work, and brainstorming how they want things to work, then you leave your IT brains in the dark and you don't get the benefit and richness of their analytical skills and technical knowledge to create even better solutions.

So, the key for you as PM is to involve your IT people enough, appropriately. Focus on your Technical Lead Analyst, and work with them to see which other IT people may need to attend which meetings.

Here are some Rules of Thumb:
- When you have key meetings in which your business analysts and SMEs are laying out and tying together the big picture of the current business situation, problems, and opportunities, you want one or two IT leads in the room as *observers*. They are there to listen, not to speak. (They hate being told to listen only—hate it, hate it, hate it! Who wouldn't?) Nonetheless, too many IT people do NOT have a good instinct for knowing what's appropriate to ask in these meetings. In my experience, it's the 80/20 rule: If IT asks questions in these early meetings, 80% of the time the question is inappropriate and pulls the meeting off course which requires additional meetings to cover lost ground. IT is invited to LISTEN in these meetings; they can ask questions of the Business Analyst (not the SMEs) afterwards.

Work Effectively with "Doer" Roles

- When you have key meetings in which your Business Analysts and SMEs are brainstorming and concluding a new Big Picture (the "To Be" business process), again, you want a couple of IT leads in the room as observers. You do not want your IT people engaging at this stage either. Their engagement here—80/20 rule—almost always shows up as "You can't do that because of XYZ technical reason."

  It is not just dangerous; it is actively harmful to have *any*one putting up roadblocks in these sessions where the business is defining what it wants and needs. It freezes creativity, and it limits possibilities. You can always down-scope a solution if it's too grandiose, time-consuming, or expensive. But, at least get very clear on what the business REALLY wants and needs before you start limiting what it will get. Your Technical Leads and your BAs (and sometimes the PM) can meet between SME sessions and discuss IT concerns and determine if any of those concerns should be addressed at this stage.

- Once the BA and SMEs have about 80% of their 'To Be' business requirements defined, then begin to fully engage your IT people. This not only adds their brainpower, knowledge, and experience to the mix for exponential value, but it also does this at a point where the business SMEs will clearly see the IT people as 'value add' instead of showstoppers. It's very fertile ground for starting good working relationships between your IT people and your SME people, who will need to interact for the duration of your project.

IDENTIFY YOUR "RIGHT HAND"

There is no official project role for the function I am about to describe here. When I use the term 'right hand,' what I mean is the one person on my team I have decided to make my backup and my most frequent sounding board.

I informally designate a right-hand person on all my large projects, and certainly on all my programs. This person is someone already on my team, in either the PM, BA, Technical Lead Analyst, or Consultant role.

The *additional* responsibilities of my right-hand person include:
- Attend key meetings with me at my request, so they are in the loop on all major project activities and issues.
- Serve as my representative in various meetings and situations. This means either:
  - The person attends a meeting on my behalf and fills me in afterwards, or
  - I fill them in on my desires and objectives beforehand and then authorize them to speak and make decisions on my behalf to achieve those.
- Serve as my backup if I'm on vacation, in a seminar, sick, or simply overbooked.
- Serve as my most reliable and capable sounding board, brainstorming, and strategic planning partner. This usually happens casually and naturally over lunch, over coffee, or in ad-hoc meetings in our offices.
- Serve as an extra set of eyes and ears for me into my team and outward into the company. Often my right-hand person will hear about issues or activities before I do, because they are closer to the source. Since they work with me so closely, they know if and when that information needs to get to me quickly.

On large projects, the amount of required thinking, strategizing, and plan 'tweaking' is enormous. I like to have one particularly excellent thinker always available to me to help me think through a particular issue, opportunity, or situation as needed. While I often have many capable thinkers and strategists on my teams, I can't keep *all* of them in the loop on all the key variables and activities of my project.

My right-hand person is the one I consciously choose to keep current. This way, I don't have to spend a lot of time giving them background information when I want to engage them in something. They are already prepped and able to work with me to quickly arrive at solutions, plans, and action items.

Work Effectively with "Doer" Roles

The challenge in having a right-hand person is balancing their workload appropriately, so they can fulfill their designated project role as well as their right-hand role. The solution usually is a simple matter of good communications between you and your right-hand person, plus planning the trickle-down delegation of their work into the team.

On rare occasions, for very large or complex projects, I may end up increasing my resource hours within the team to account for this trickle-down work. For example, I may request an extra 20% time allocation for a Technical Lead Analyst, if my right-hand person plans to delegate some work to that analyst in order to free up their time to work more closely with me. Since I plan for my right-hand role from the start, these extra resource hours are accounted for in my initial resource request.

BUSINESS PROCESS IMPLEMENTERS

Business Process Implementers are a group of people that are rarely acknowledged in a project; this is because their work typically relates to the 'out of scope' activities discussed in the BA section of this chapter.

In most project organizational charts, *all* hands-on business people are clumped together and called SMEs. The role of SME, however, is usually limited to giving business expertise to the team, participating in the solution design, and participating in user testing of that solution once it's been developed.

When a project will result in changes to the operational 'things people do' daily in the business—what reports they see, what screens they touch, what people and groups they talk to, which customers they interact with—then business resources must prepare all impacted people for those changes. That preparation consists of creating or changing policies, procedures, tools, roles and responsibilities, staffing and staffing allocation, job-specific training, and so on.

Designing these items and putting them into effect *is* business process implementation. The people who do this work are Business Process Implementers. These activities must be coordinated with all the other project implementation activities to achieve a seamless project rollout.

If this work is not done, then your project will only deliver system changes and minimal training. The business people will not be ready to take advantage of all the new changes, so the project results will be less than they could be, AND the business reaction to your project will be pain, struggle, annoyance, and ultimately failure.

Historically, managing this business process implementation work has been the responsibility of Stakeholders and line managers outside the project. [*See "Stakeholders" role description in Chapter 4.*] Historically, these people don't have a Big Picture understanding of projects, and they don't have the benefit of knowing project management methods and tools. So, this business process implementation work is often addressed poorly, and too late.

This work must get done either within or alongside your project. Get clear on who owns this, and then coordinate yourselves via some structured communications. If you own it, and I recommend you do for large projects, manage the people in this role through your Stakeholders, Business Analysts, and SMEs.

DEVELOPERS/ PROGRAMMER ANALYSTS

Typical responsibilities of Developers and Programmer Analysts include:
- Create the detailed solution design.
- Ensure the technical design maps to the documented business requirements.
- Develop the solution.
- Unit test the solution (test each piece of the solution).
- System test the solution (test how all the pieces work together).
- Support the business user testing.

Work Effectively with "Doer" Roles

In large projects, it is rare that you will work directly with your developers. They will usually be managed by your Technical Lead Analysts and/or a matrixed Technical Project Manager.

If you have a small- to mid-sized project, you are the PM, so you will be working with Developers. The main item to watch out for with your Developers is to keep them to the plan. Once a person gets their hands into a program, or a set of programs, they find lots of things they did not expect. Each new thing is a trail your Developer can follow. Each one they follow, eats up their time. Therefore, you need to have many routine management interventions to discover which trails your Developers are following, so you can approve or disapprove that time and effort.

The nature of Developers is to be problem solvers. Each trail is a problem to be solved. This intervention is really just you saying, "Yes, this problem needs to be solved" or "No, that's not a problem relative to this project and our priorities—let it be."

I'm using the term 'intervention' here because that's the effect you are creating. What you are actually doing is simply following good project management practices: You will have a detailed project plan with each Developer's tasks and due dates assigned to guide them; you will make sure each Developer understands and commits to that plan, their tasks, and their due dates, and then you will meet with them twice a week, weekly, or daily for them to give you their current status on each task.

Closing Tip:

This concludes the topic of roles and responsibilities. This is a lot of information; don't forget that a short bulleted chart containing the definition of all these typical project roles and responsibilities is available on our website: *www.ProjectLeadershipGold.com.*

CHAPTER SIX

HIGH-VOLTAGE RESOURCE PLANNING

The nature of a project team makes it a unique entity to manage and staff. It is generally an ad-hoc collection of people thrown together quickly, who may or may not even know each other, and who may or may not ever have done the jobs they are now assigned to do.

The "thrown-together team" presents two types of challenges for the PM:

1. Sufficiency of resources
2. Initiation of resources

The challenge of sufficiency is making sure there are enough qualified people, in the right positions, on the team. The challenge of initiation is making sure all these people get on board *quickly*, armed with the right information to begin their work quickly and well.

Own the Forest, Delegate the Trees

For <u>sufficiency</u> of resources, PMs need to be able to answer "Yes" to each of these questions:
- Do I have the right people, with the right skills?
- Do I have enough dedicated[15] people?
- Do I have enough time from my matrixed people?

For the <u>initiation</u> of resources into the project, PMs need to achieve at least the following items within the first week or two of the project:
- Meet one-on-one with your Sponsor, key leads (internal to your company and external), and any pivotal Stakeholders whose active support you require.
- Collect their high-level "must have" needs and objectives.
- Discuss your needs and expectations of their participation, and achieve mutual agreement.
- Develop the project organization chart, showing roles, responsibilities, and relationships.
- Develop a high-level project timeline, identifying a definite kickoff date on which you'll provide ALL the information your team needs to get started.[16]

In this chapter, we'll cover all these items except for the project organization chart, which was covered in Chapter 3.

---

[15] Dedicated people are assigned to work your project on a full-time basis. They aren't borrowed; they are *given* to you, usually for the duration of the project.

[16] Some project standards don't require a timeline this early in the game. In my experience, your Sponsor, executives and entire team will want you to provide a timeline at this point as a framework for "what's next." Plus, I need it to kick myself into full gear; seeing the timeline this early really highlights the urgency of getting the project in motion immediately.

SUFFICIENCY

Your objective with sufficiency is to make sure you are appropriately staffed to get the job done. I believe having the right team is your most important responsibility. Many PMs don't seem to understand they have options here and that it is their responsibility to get appropriate staffing.

If you're an active PM, then you can probably relate to this typical example of how a team gets formed: There are somewhere between three and ten mid-to-senior executives in a room somewhere, guessing about your resource needs, based on their own experience plus some early input from you. They look into their own organizations, decide who they want to give to the project, and—voilà!—your team is born.

Now, some of these people will be great. They'll be exactly who you would have chosen. In fact, some of them may be exactly who you DID choose. However, you probably do not even know some of the other people who are now on your team. The bigger the project and the broader its scope, the more of these unknowns you will have.

To assess the team, you need to do some sleuthing. You need to explore the talent and effectiveness of your new team just as trial lawyers need to explore the openness and potential effectiveness of their jury. Of course, you have much less time to do this.

STRATEGIC SUFFICIENCY SESSION

I recommend you do an assessment quickly and from your gut. If you have a big team, then do this assessment with your top two or three leads, and focus on the people in key project positions. For example, whether you have a 1,000-person team or a 300-person team, as the leader you are most concerned at this point with getting the best possible people into the key five to fifteen positions on your team.

This whole process, even on a large project, should take about two to three hours. Remember this is a from-the-gut assessment. It has to be at this point, because the only information you have about the quality of your assigned people is the personal experience of the people in this meeting, plus whatever you may have heard through the company grapevine.[17]

Remember that these people have already been assigned to you; no one is giving you the luxury of launching your own interview process so you can pick and choose who you want. Usually, no one is even expecting you to question your assigned resources; most PMs do not. They accept whom they're given because that is the management expectation.

If you have accepted 100% accountability for delivering your project on time, then you cannot afford to bypass this opportunity to plug performance and skill gaps that could otherwise derail your project. This work session is your attempt to quickly unearth any gross mis-assignments, so you can deal with them before your project starts.

While company gossip is a pretty unreliable information source in general, it can have value to you in this case. Really great people tend to be known as great, and really ineffective people tend to be known as ineffective. You are looking for performance extremes at this point:

- *If this work session* indicates you have a fairly strong set of people in your key roles, fine, then you'll accept those assignments.
- *If this work session* indicates you have a fairly medium set of people in your key roles, then you are missing strength and initiative, and you'll need to get at least a couple of those assignments switched and bring in superior talent.
- *If this work session* indicates you have one or more poor or very questionable people in your key roles, then you will need to probe that information and either supplant or buttress those people with superior talent.

---

[17] It sounds funny to list the company grapevine as one information source, but if I listen to my trusted cohort Sam and he tells me assigned-person Bob is fabulous, then I will tend to be glad Bob has been assigned to my project and I will want to keep him. If Sam tells me he heard that Bob is a non-productive slug, then I will ask whom he heard that from, and if I trust that source, I will tend to question Bob's assignment to my project and I will dig deeper with an eye towards possibly removing Bob if keeping him is too risky. I think most managers do this kind of informal performance checking from time to time, even though the information is not exactly reliable. Our alternatives are either managing blind or managing from possible misinformation; both alternatives are risky.

High-Voltage Resource Planning

Necessary steps:

- Draft your project organization chart (*see Chapters 3 through 5*).
- Map each assigned person to their most likely role on the project.
- Identify any people you flat out don't want on your team. You must have valid business reasons for this. Valid business reasons include:
  » You have personal experience with this person and know they do not have the skills.
  » The position is too pivotal for you to have a questionable resource; you need an ace in that role from the start.
  » You have too many chiefs on your team and need a lower-level person who will get their hands dirty.
  » Your team is weak overall in a particular skill set, for example, business analysis, and you need at least one of your slots filled with a senior Business Analyst expert who can lead and guide the others.
- Identify your desired solution for any person you want added or exchanged. Whom do you want instead? Will the person be internal or external? If you know you're asking for one of the company's best people (and I recommend you do this if you and your management are serious about getting this project done on time and well), then be prepared to explain why it's in the company's best interest for this person to be on your team versus whatever else they are slotted for.

Here's how this played out while I was working at Freddie Mac (Federal Home Loan Mortgage Company) on an 18-month program to implement an entirely new daily working process for one department. While I did not know what all those work changes would be at a detailed level, I did know the macro scope of those changes for the department, and it seemed very large. By the time the program was complete, that department would be:

- Processing five million additional transactions each month,
- Balancing all that data in new ways, using new reports and new interactive screens,
- Reconciling that data each month with thousands of customers, each of whom also would be using new data, new reports, and balancing new items, and

- Managing this additional monthly data within a shorter processing window, from eight days down to seven days.

Our plan was to implement these changes through a series of projects, with several projects in progress at a time, each in various stages of completion.

I was initially assigned two SMEs on a part-time basis to represent the 100+ person department. When my leads and I conducted the resource sufficiency work session as described above, we pooled our information and concluded that the two people who had been assigned seemed to be excellent, but we needed to validate that. We also concluded that two Subject Matter Experts were not enough; we needed three Subject Matter Experts, full-time. They needed to be three of the absolute best, brightest, most creative, and forward-thinking people that department had.

When I went to the department head to request the additional person and validate the excellence of the other two, I explained my rationale in this way: "Everything your people do in their eight hours each day will be different once this project is done. We'll do our best with whatever people you give us, but if you want this project to create the best possible future work processes and supporting systems for your department, then you need to put your best people on this team."

No department can easily release its top three people to any project; it creates a huge and painful gap in ongoing operations (*see Chapter 16 "Track and Resolve Resource Constraints" for help strategizing and negotiating resource changes*). This argument worked, both because it was true and because I was communicating my staffing needs from a "What's best for the business?" standpoint, rather than a "What's best for my project?" standpoint.

TEAM MEMBER TIME ALLOCATION

After you have identified the people you want to keep and those people you want to add or exchange, you need to have one more piece of information before you go out and begin your resource negotiations. You need to determine how much time you need from each team resource.

First, identify those people you need on a full-time dedicated basis. Usually, you will need your key leads to be full-time; they have co-leadership responsibilities with and for you, plus they have management accountabilities to the people reporting to them in the project organization chart.

You want 100% of their time, focus, and attention on your project. You want key people to be thinking about your project when they drive to work in the morning, when they have lunch in the cafeteria, when they drive home at night, and when they're at happy hour with their buddies. Much of the creative, driving work of a project happens in this off-hours thinking time.

You need more than just yourself doing this work. Never be the only full-time dedicated resource on your project.

I already mentioned this rule of thumb: Once you have about five direct reports, you need to be a full-time PM. I'll add to that a rule of thumb regarding dedicated resources: No fewer than three and, ideally, four or more full-time, dedicated leads should be assigned to a medium project of about 20 to 30 people. This is about a 12% to 13% ratio of dedicated-to-non-dedicated resource staffing (excluding you as the overall dedicated PM). These leads usually report directly into the PM, and the rest of the team reports directly into these leads.

When I use the term 'lead' here, I am referring to a role or function, not necessarily to a title. For example, I can designate a Business Analyst, Project Manager, Technical Analyst, Consultant, or even a SME as a lead in my project—if they have the management and leadership skills I need. I look for these qualities and abilities in people I place in lead roles within my teams:

"Get" things quickly – *They don't need much information to get the right things done well, and they won't settle for less information than they need.*	**Fun to work with** – *Have personal energy and enthusiasm for the work, laugh a lot, and don't take things personally.*	**Creative and positive** – *They assume solutions are possible and that they will find them.*
Experienced in their role – *They don't need detailed guidance because the depth of their experience fills in the gaps.*	**Well-respected** *within the company, within their peer group for their knowledge and expertise*	**Savvy communicators** – *They have a good sense for what information is appropriate to share with whom, at what level of detail.*
Reliable communicators – *Know what's important to communicate, and are able to communicate it well.*	**Dependable** – *When they say they will do something, it gets done, and done well.*	**Excellent work ethics** – *They are living examples of personal productivity, commitment, and focus.*
Have **tremendous initiative**, *and employ it within the parameters of PM directives.*	**Honest, confident, trustworthy** – *They deal in facts and reality; no game-playing; no hidden agendas.*	**Accountable** – *They take pride in their work, and they stand behind it.*

In general, the shorter the timeline, the more dedicated resources you need. And, the more complex the project, the more dedicated resources you will need, so each key aspect of the project gets needed attention and creative leadership brainpower.

As noted earlier, people who are not dedicated 100% to your project are matrixed resources. By definition, this means their number-one priority is NOT you or your project; *their priority is pleasing and meeting the needs of their line manager.* This is true even if the person is matrixed to you on a 70% to 80% basis. As long as they have some other project, task, or function they must do (aside from administration), that other item can eclipse your project at that line manager's discretion.

I am intensely wary of time commitments for any resource assigned to me less than 50%. (*The exceptions to this are the key Stakeholders and the Subject Matter Experts whose situational expertise I need only on an occasional basis.*) I always want the most critical Subject Matter Experts, those upon whom I rely for their comprehensive understanding of the relevant business process(es), MORE than 50%. On really large projects, I want them dedicated.

For my key resources, I also want heavily weighted input into their performance reviews, so their income and future assignments and promotability are proportionately tied to how well they do on my project.

Here is why a less-than-50% allocation so often fails:

- Human nature is such that both you and the person's line manager will both attempt to task this person 100% anyway, creating a situation in which all three of you will lose.

- Human nature also dictates that if it comes to making a choice between pleasing you or pleasing a line manager, then the person will choose the one who has the most impact on salary, bonuses, performance reviews, and job security. In a matrix situation, you lose.

- People in this situation inevitably find their energy and attention is fragmented between the project and all other work. It takes more time and effort on your part to keep such team members up-do-date on what's happening in the project. They, in turn, lose track and lose momentum switching back and forth.

- People whose time is fragmented miss meetings. Your project is now subject to the whims and inefficiencies of whatever else is going on in their non-project time. When emergencies crop up in those areas, your project suffers.

The worse case I ever saw of this was when I was working as a consultant to one Fortune 500 company during a time period in which they started and concluded buy-out negotiations with another Fortune 500 company. People who had been assigned to my project suddenly began skipping project meetings because they were getting pulled by their line managers into meetings related to implementing the buy-out. The impact to my project was that even though the company originally *committed* more resources than we'd requested, after 90 days the program had only received 60% of the resources we needed.

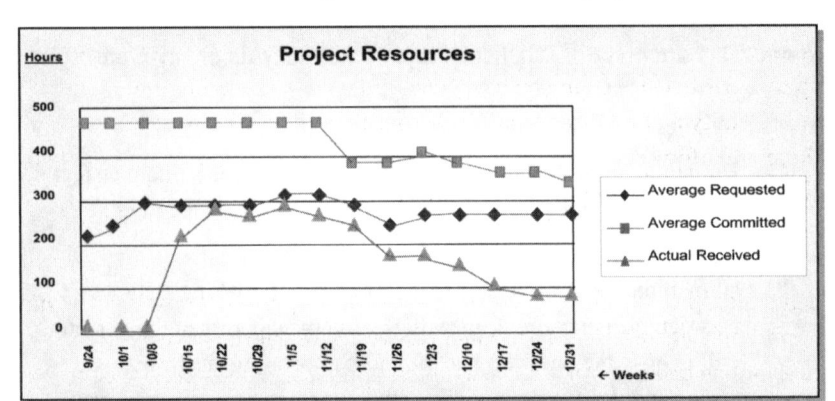

Here is the actual data showing this resource hit to the project:

Project Resources

(Chart showing Hours vs. Weeks from 9/24 to 12/31, with three series: Average Requested, Average Committed, and Actual Received)

This chart shows what happens when a company avoids committing *dedicated* resources, and tries to make up for it by committing extra *matrixed* resources. For this project, on paper it looks like we were given more resources than we requested. In practice, this just introduced many more people with tiny time commitments.

The smaller the time commitment, the lower our project sat within each individual's priority list. Missed meetings and delayed meetings became rampant. Within this 90-day window, we had only one three-week period where we operated at full strength.

It is worth noting that even with this chronic 40% matrixed resource shortfall, our project suffered only a 20% delay in deliverables. The reason is we still had *dedicated* resources in the most critical positions, and they were able to create all sorts of workaround solutions that helped us make substantial progress in the face of otherwise overwhelming resource losses.

USING MASTERMIND TEAMS

No matter what size team you have, one of the very first things you want to do is identify and establish what I call your project "mastermind teams."[18] These are informal management clusters within your overall team, each with a targeted focus on one slice of the project.

Within these clusters, while project roles and responsibilities are clearly maintained, the 'feeling' of the working relationship is one of partnership and purposeful camaraderie. Mastermind partners have enormous respect and trust for one another. They have an unstated mutual dependence on each other to get the job done, and they will not let the others down.

Mastermind teams tend to be triads with three partners. As PM, you are often one of these partners. This concept of mastermind teams can be confusing; let me start explaining it by giving you some examples of powerful mastermind teams I've had on various projects.

While I was working in a direct-mail marketing company, Credit Card Service Corporation, I was the technical PM for the launch of a new direct mail travel product. Three mastermind teams evolved quickly in that project:

- **Strategic mastermind team** *(PM plus two Business Analysts)*: We were the core leaders designing the change, communicating the design to the corporation, sharing plans, and engaging all the business and technical people required to create and implement the product, testing, and training.

- **Technical mastermind team** *(PM, Senior Systems Analyst, lead external contractor)*: We were the core leaders of the technical side of the project plan. I instituted the plans and structure; the systems analyst drove it down through the internal technical team, and the contractor drove it down through the external team.

---

[18] The term "mastermind" is not new, though I haven't seen anyone else use it for projects. The oldest source I've seen for this term is Napoleon Hill's book *Think and Grow Rich*. Paraphrasing, Napoleon defines mastermind groups as people coming together to work towards a common objective in a spirit of perfect harmony, during the course of which they create and have access to a force that is greater than the sum of their individual contributions.

- *Problem-Solving mastermind team (PM, PM Director, fellow PMs)*: We met weekly and on an ad-hoc basis. These were my tactical project management operations partners, helping me raise and resolve general project issues, and working with me to obtain the resources I needed.

These three mastermind teams enabled me to tap into a deep talent pool, via very few people and interactions. Through them, I was successfully able to manage a project team of 15 dedicated people and 20 part-time matrixed people.

I had several mastermind teams for the Freddie Mac project I mentioned earlier. Some mastermind teams evolved quickly. Some evolved after a few months. For this project, I was the PM leading from within the business operations division.

- *Leadership mastermind team (PM, Sponsor, IT Director)*: This was the core leadership triad. It's where key project needs and decisions were raised, agreed on, and promoted to the right decision-makers.
- *Technical mastermind team (PM, IT Director, lead IT PM):* Together, we managed and drove the IT aspects of the program. We broke the work into six sub-projects, established a phased approach, and created the business and IT personnel pairings that made the whole thing work.
- *Business operations management mastermind team (PM, Sponsor, key business Stakeholder)*: Through this group, I was able to keep my eye on the business operations ball, and keep my team there. I was able to escalate issues and obtain rapid business decisions, and educate and influence the business projects that were needed to help internal customer service departments handle the new processes, jobs, and technical system tools.
- *Business process re-engineering mastermind team (PM, consultant partner, lead consultants)*: At the point we first realized the massive *business operations* implications of what had started as a technical project, my Sponsor and I brought external Change Management consultants on board. We were doing business process reengineering before that concept became widely known, and we needed help.

High-Voltage Resource Planning

These consultants were key to help me see what I was actually dealing with, and to help me bring in and implement the best practices to effect change on this scale. Remember, as PM, it's not your responsibility to know everything; it's your responsibility to see what's needed and to go get it.

- ***Business Analysts team** (PM, three top Business Analysts)*: Through this group, I was able to see into the daily workings of each project team. Together, we made sure that business requirements were thorough, well documented, and clearly understood, and we established effective routines and mechanisms to ensure that business, technical, and customer SMEs worked well together to achieve coordinated results.

- ***Training mastermind team** (PM, Lead Trainer, Sponsor)*: This team was formed to divert department training staff to prepare training materials for internal and external customers, to help customers be able to use the new systems we were implementing.

- ***Daily business operations mastermind team** (PM, Business Director, Lead Business SMEs)*: I loved this group. This got me closest to the business, and helped me see how the six phased technical project implementations created six phases of operations change for our business customers. Through this team, the business ended up adding about 30 accountants to the department and moved from working standard business days to 24/7 work shifts to handle the extra workload.

I never met half the people who worked on this program, yet I was able to manage the program and all its resources effectively through the leverage these mastermind teams gave me. Through these teams, I had leadership access to the skills, talents, and abilities of 200 or so people.

As you can see, mastermind teams are a great mechanism through which you can *delegate the trees*. This is the value of creating mastermind teams. These teams leverage your time, give you quick and broad communications access to all players on your team, and prevent you from being your team's biggest bottleneck. A side benefit: When you use masterminds, you are also creating personnel backups.

Own the Forest, Delegate the Trees

Masterminding is a form of delegation that gives you a huge ability to influence, guide, and direct the core solutions and activities of your team. It does this while freeing you from the details, so you can keep managing the Big Picture and keep looking ahead for your team.

> *The whole topic of creating effective teams through designing the right project organization structure, and then finding, engaging, focusing and engaging the right people, is very logical and common-sense. But, it still can be complex to apply all this information rapidly and well within the initial start-up of a project. We can help you do this: My company offers workshop-style training and coaching programs in which we will work with you on the specifics of your projects, and help you apply the information in this book and make the on-the-job changes that will immediately increase your success. For more information, please check out our website, and use our Contact Us page to ask us any questions you may have:*
> *www.ProjectLeadershipGold.com*

Section III: Essential Start-Up Success Strategies

CHAPTER SEVEN

TIME-TESTED STRUCTURE AND ROUTINE

Most people dislike having to abide by structure and routine, yet projects don't work without these. Structure and routine are core tools and deliverables of the PM. It's your job to make the routines productive. People will not honor structure for long unless they see value in it. You are responsible for implementing effective procedures and routines on your project and ensuring all players work within them.

The larger, more complex, or more urgent the project, the more vital structure becomes.

You need to understand that your team members will tend to resist structure. People become very nimble and creative when they're trying to avoid things they don't like.

It's your job to help your team follow the structure and to hold their feet to the fire, if necessary, if they don't. Setting a good example is a requirement: Be on time for meetings, follow through on commitments, and so on. Clear and consistent communication and effective leadership are other key tools to gain people's commitment to structure.

I have a love-hate relationship with structure.

It's always funny to me when people say, "You're so organized" and "You're always on top of the details." I really don't like this stuff. But, I do it. And, I make sure my teams do it.

Very large projects likely involve thousands of individual tasks, performed by hundreds of people, from dozens of different organizational units or companies. These tasks all need to take place within a limited time frame and in a specific sequence. Most tasks are dependent in some way on other tasks.

Without structure, this would all be sheer chaos. As the PM, you are the person responsible both for seeing this whole picture and for developing and implementing the right structure to make this project work.

The elements of project structure covered in this chapter include:
- Roles and Responsibilities
- Project Schedule
- The Project Plan

COMMUNICATE DEFINED ROLES AND RESPONSIBILITIES

You may have thought I've beaten this topic to death already in Chapters 4 and 5, but nope, I've got more to say!

I attended a Breakthrough to Success seminar led by Jack Canfield, bestselling author of *The Principles of Success*. In that eight-day seminar, Jack led the group in several exercises. For one exercise, Jack spent maybe three minutes giving us clear, step-by-step instructions for how to do the exercise. After three minutes, Jack asked if anyone had questions about the exercise.

People asked questions for 30 minutes!

I was amazed. It seemed so simple, yet this audience of highly skilled business-savvy professionals had 30 minutes worth of questions. As I listened, I could tell some people were just confused; some people hadn't been paying attention, and some people had a logical but different interpretation of what Jack had said from what I had heard. Once all the questions were asked and answered, the exercise itself went quickly and flawlessly.

It got me thinking about myself as a leader, and how often I give my team 'clear' direction.

The point I learned from watching Jack is this: People need far more clarity about what you expect from them than you think. As leaders, you and I need to lay things out clearly and with great detail, and then invite questions, and patiently answer each and every one.

It is not my team's role to guess what I want and need from them. It's my role to make these things clear and to verify that my team members understand. Once they understand, *then* they are able to use their initiative and get the job done. Any time I've tried to short-step this, it's come back to haunt me.

Defined roles and responsibilities are one of the best tools you have to divide and conquer the workload. You want people out of each other's hair and out of each other's business as much as possible. In this way, you can help ensure that each member of your team stays appropriately focused on the work for which he or she is personally responsible.

There are some people on every project who keep looking over the fence into other parts of the project where they don't belong. If left unchecked, pretty soon their own work is left undone, and they are stirring up confusion in some other aspect of your project. People usually do this because they see something that needs doing, so they involve themselves to help get it done. The intention is good, but the result is harmful to the project.

Clear roles and responsibilities give these people boundaries. They don't have to worry about what's going on across the fence; it's someone else's job. Clear roles and responsibilities also let them know, "You *are* accountable for *this*." When people truly understand what they will be held personally and publicly accountable for, they'll usually decide it's big enough to keep them focused.

PROJECT SCHEDULE

You usually know a couple of things about your project at the start: You know your goal, and you know your due date. With those two pieces of information, you can create a project schedule that defines the highest-level phases of your project.

Start planning by looking at the finish. Work backwards from your project due date and establish interim due dates for each of your high-level phases. The following is a sample high-level project schedule, using generic problem-solving steps as phases:

Sample Project Schedule

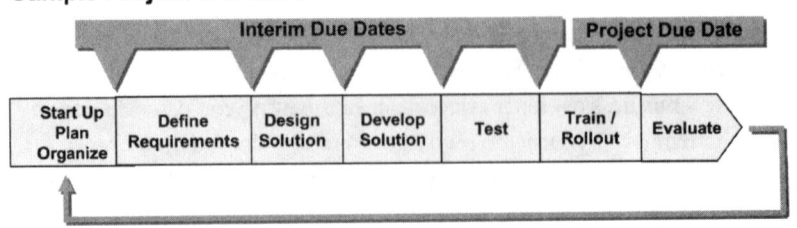

Start Up Plan Organize	Define Requirements	Design Solution	Develop Solution	Test	Train / Rollout	Evaluate

Interim Due Dates | Project Due Date

This schedule is a critical structural component of your project. It tells the team some of the most important information they need to know: when they need to get things done.

The plan details fit within the schedule, and generally speaking, more detail is available for the early phases. Later-phase *details* are vague until the work of the first few phases is nearing completion. The later-phase *schedule* can be guessed at quite early, because you already know the desired due date, so you can work backwards from there.

The project plan and schedule give this initial structure to your project:
- The overall start-to-finish is solid and well understood.
- The phase starts and finishes are pretty solid as well, though you may shift weeks between phases as detail becomes known. If any phase end date is missed, then the whole project is at instant high risk.

Once people know their own roles and responsibilities and they see this schedule, they can get an immediate sense of the relative urgency of their work. From this, they can see the pace they need to set for themselves. As PM, it's your responsibility to make this information clear to all project parties to be sure they do grasp what is needed.

PROJECT PLAN

The value of a project plan as a tool to help you structure the work of your team is pretty clear. The project plan is your single, most powerful tool to proactively manage due date pressure.

The first thing you and your leads will do after receiving approval on your initial project approach, phasing, and rough schedule is get your plan to a working level of detail. Depending on the project, this could add hundreds or even thousands of task lines to your plan. My rule of thumb is to own the plans, but to delegate the writing of the plan whenever possible to the project manager closest to the actual work.

Obviously, if you're the only project manager, this means you. However, for the large projects and programs, you'll have one or more project managers reporting to you. It's important that they create their own plans, with their leads. You need their ownership and commitment to the detailed plans, and the only way to get that is to have them do it.

I sit in on all project-planning meetings. I only failed to do this on one program, and the resulting plans were disastrous—we ended up with plans that were not specific, and that did not include deliverables. It took way too much management overhead time to make sure things stayed on track. So—sit in on all project planning sessions, and make sure the resulting plans are logical, clear, and that they contain all the necessary elements, including:

- Phases
- Tasks
- Dependencies
- Key deliverables
- Assignments (always designate an owner, even if multiple people are working the task or if the resource is not yet acquired, i.e. Resource 1, Resource 2, etc.)
- Task due dates

I see lots of articles and discussions regarding project planning tools and software, and my advice to you is: Choose one and move on. A good project plan is all about content; you just want a tool to help you make that content clear. The tool is an aid; it's not the deliverable.

I've used several different types of software, but mostly Microsoft Project simply because that's what most of my clients and companies have used. It can be challenging to update, but it remains an extremely powerful tool to help initially set up a clean, logical, and detailed project plan. Excel is my second choice; it's okay, but you can't easily see dependencies, and it isn't easy to view the information in different ways.

I don't have hard and fast rules about how to write my project plans, other than requiring the elements above. My plans often are different from program to program. I've never used sub-projects, though I've attempted it a couple of times. For me, it's ended up being quicker and cleaner to have multiple project plans, with a single Level One plan to tie it all together.

I always start with the due date,[19] and work backwards from there. *(See Chapter 8 "Master Your Due Dates" for strategic thinking, negotiations, and use of assigned due dates.)*

Identify the phases, and estimate duration and stop-start dates per phase. This is pretty much my Level One plan. Then, I take each phase and break it into the five to seven major tasks and deliverables needed in that phase. This is my Level Two plan.

For each phase, I then break it down into the level of detail required to actually assign tasks to individuals. The result is a Level Three or Four plan. This is the lowest level of detail I'll ever manage to; my leads may break sections down even further, but I don't need visibility into that as long as each honors my higher-level plan.

There are exceptions to everything though, which is what makes project management so challenging. A few years ago, I was an executive consultant to Hilton Hotels Corporation, serving as the program manager for a data center move. Hilton was moving their data center for some core applications from California to Memphis. This involved tasks like procuring replicated hardware and software for the Memphis site from over 100 different vendors, installing each, testing each, transmitting live data from one site to the other, and so on. The applications included a 'hotel reservations' system, which was a revenue-generating vehicle the company could not afford to shut down for long. In fact, we were given only two possible 48-hour windows in the year in which we could shut that application down to implement the cutover.

We had pages and pages of detailed project plans for that 48-hour period alone. On top of that, we had a Y2K-type[20] communications mechanism established, so everyone could know exactly how the cutover was progressing. It took two long, frustrating, mind-numbing days for 12 of us to painstakingly

---

[19] When I talk about always "starting with the due date," I am talking about the *thinking* process of planning a project. I am *not* suggesting or recommending anything regarding how best to translate that information for data entry into a tool such as Microsoft Office Project. You will need to look to other sources (such as your tool vendor) for that kind of information.

[20] Y2K stands for 'Year 2000.' Within the project world, the term Y2K generally referred to all projects across the globe that were launched to update any computer program that could 'break' due to incorrect date calculations when the centuries switched from 1999 to 2000.

develop these detailed plans. But, they worked like a charm! That level of detailed planning simply had to be done. The complexity of the tasks, the sheer quantity of players, the dependencies and sequencing of the tasks, and the tiny execution window all dictated the need for precision planning.

Most projects don't need anything like this, but it's important for you to remember that project management and project plans are not rigid, paint-by-number disciplines. They are a marriage of generic thinking, strategy, structure, and tools ... coupled with common sense, creative thinking, commitment, and effective application of human talent and ingenuity.

For programs, which are generally large, complex, and involve dozens and maybe hundreds of people, I usually only create detail plans (Levels Three and Four) for each phase on a "just in time" basis. This is for two reasons: 1) There are too many unknowns to make the effort of detail planning for later phases worthwhile, and 2) The need to get people into motion, effectively and rapidly, is immediate and urgent and to do that you need to be putting your plans into motion fast.

So, now you have detailed plans in place for at least your current phase and the next phase beyond the current phase.

By the way, I see a lot of people treat a project plan as if it's cast in concrete. In many cases, that can work against you. When a methodology treats the plan as the Holy Grail, I know it was developed by people who don't understand the game of managing large projects.

Remember, some of the key features of a project include:
- People who are new to this work, and
- People who are new to their role.

The project itself often covers work the company has never done before, such as developing a brand-new product, redesigning a process, merging a company, outsourcing a function, or closing a facility.

Any plan created for these circumstances is bound to change over time, simply because there are so many unknowns and variables at the start.

One of the greatest writers of all time on the topic of success is Napoleon Hill, who wrote the classic *Think and Grow Rich* book about 85 years ago. Mr. Hill studied the most successful business legends at the height of the Industrial Revolution, including Henry Ford, Nelson Rockefeller, Dale Carnegie, and Albert Einstein, and this is what he found on the topic of plans:

> *"The majority of men meet with failure because of their lack of persistence in creating new plans to take the place of those which fail."*

MAKE YOUR STRUCTURE SUCCESSFUL

The most important thing you can do to get your team to adhere to the structures you put in place is to rigorously adhere to the structure yourself. Be on time, start meetings on time, respond timely to e-mails and phone calls, honor your commitments, and visibly follow your plan and schedule.

The second most important thing you can do is hold your team accountable for adhering to structure. If they are late for a meeting, or they miss a scheduled phone call—call them on it. Let them know you noticed, remind them of the structure, and confirm their commitment to show up on time going forward.

If you want to be seen as the nice guy, then you're in the wrong role. I'm not telling you it's okay to be mean or disrespectful. It's important that you be respectful in how you do things. But, don't choose to do things or not because you want someone to like you. Calling someone on a missed meeting or any failure is not being mean; it is simply doing the job you are being held responsible for as the PM.

Calling people on missed meetings and late attendance is a point of leadership. People may dislike structure, and sometimes they resent or reject it. But, people do like to be and feel successful. You know structure is imperative; few people on your team will see this imperative as clearly as you do. They don't have to know structure is imperative; that's your job. The corollary is that you must impose structure and work with the individuals who resist it until they work it out.

Here is a little tried and true verbiage that is short, respectful, and gets the job done:

Sample "Hey, you missed a meeting" Call

"Hi, Bob. It's Barb. I understand you weren't able to make our XYZ meeting this morning and that it's been re-scheduled for Thursday. I'm just calling to check in to see if anything's going on with your availability that I need to know about."

You've made your point; they know you're keeping tabs and that they'll be hearing from you if they miss meetings. Now listen to their answer. You need to understand if this could grow into a bigger issue:

"So, this was just a one-time thing?"

If 'Yes':

"Great! Thanks for your time. See you Thursday."

If they indicate (or you recognize) this may not be a one-time thing:

"No? You think you might be missing more meetings? What can I do or who do I need to talk to, so we can make sure you're able to attend these meetings?"

Continue the conversation until you are clear on what action you need to take to clear whatever obstacles are in the way of this person attending your meetings.

The third most important thing you can do regarding implementing structure is *don't* impose structure that is not valuable. Sometimes you can't help this. For example, your company or PMO (Program Management Office) may require certain things to occur in your project, and you agreed to comply. (Note: Unless you raise any of these as issues and successfully negotiate the right to an exception, you *have* implicitly agreed to comply.[21])

Mostly though, the communication structures in your process come from you. When you schedule routine meetings, make sure they are valuable to all participants. If they are not, then you may have the wrong participants, or you may need to change the meeting or drop it. When you require written communications, such as updates to the plan, status e-mails, or reports, make sure you actually need and use that information. If you don't have time to use it, then you probably don't need it.

A FINAL WORD ABOUT STRUCTURE

You are the person who established the schedule, plans, and structures for your project. You are the person who demonstrates how seriously you take these. Your actions tell your team how seriously they need to take them.

People will generally give you a bit of leeway at the start of your project. They know you are their leader, and they expect you to set some ground rules and procedures. They will usually follow along for a very short period of time out of human kindness and respect for your role. But, they need to see and experience the value of your structure very quickly, because most people's natural inclination is towards freedom and away from structure. They will be looking for reasons to ignore your structure and follow their own way of doing things.

---

[21] The exception to such implicit compliance would be the case where you consciously and deliberately decide to ignore a guideline. I covered this earlier in Chapter 5. I add here: When you choose to bypass compliance, you are taking on the risk that some authority could always overrule you. In such cases, your project could take a hit, and you would be held accountable.

Own the Forest, Delegate the Trees

If you can understand and accept this as a general behavior pattern of your team, then you can be creatively flexible in tweaking your structure as needed to get the job done. Making these "tweaks" and being willing to make change to your plan and the structure based on the needs of the project are a clear manner of demonstrating your personal commitment to both.

CHAPTER EIGHT

MASTER YOUR DUE-DATES

Due dates are a real sore point with many PMs and, therefore, for many team members as well. As we all know, due dates often seem to be plucked from the ether. They reflect the business's desire, not necessarily the reality. Initial due dates are rarely set with the knowledge of what it will take to meet that date.

TREAT YOUR GIVEN DUE-DATE AS SET IN STONE

If I'm given the chance to participate in setting the due date in the first place, I do mention and write my simple caveat: "This date is only a guesstimate; we haven't done the analysis yet to validate this solution or workload."

Corporate planning is a dance between business wants and needs, and the operational and opportunity costs of those wants and needs. Project "Go/No Go" decisions must be made, and most of those decisions will be "No." It makes no sense for a company to invest a lot in the up-front, "What will it really take?" analysis of *all* of the proposed projects.

Own the Forest, Delegate the Trees

Your company most likely has some formal rules and practices around estimating project timelines and resource needs. The resulting estimates are still essentially the best guesses of experienced people using structured techniques.

Everyone knows these dates are guesses. Don't get tangled up in arguing these initial due dates at the outset; you can waste a lot of time and energy that way. Instead, just state your caveat and put it in writing somewhere, and then do your best to find a way to meet the company's desired date.

As the assigned PM, the accuracy of my *assigned* due date is not my concern. My task is to meet that assigned due date, or to demonstrate why I can't meet it, and propose a couple of viable options that meet the business objectives as fast as possible, at the lowest possible cost.

Here's my general approach to do this:

Regardless of how viable I think it is, I first accept any due date I'm given as set in stone. This means I treat it as *the* key fixed variable during solution planning, analysis, and negotiations.

I then work with my team to develop a viable plan to meet that due date, and prove to ourselves how it can be done. Changing the due date is an absolute last resort, *not even open for discussion* unless my team has already done intense, exhaustive research and proven to me that an in-date solution is impossible and/or too costly.

A lot of project managers do *not* just accept the given due date as a challenge and work aggressively with it. They get stuck on the perceived unfairness of the date or the perceived lack of reality behind it. What these project managers do then is go through the *motions* of project management. They put together a plan they don't believe in. They present it to their Sponsor with a huge list of caveats. When they execute their plan, it fails; then, they point to all their caveats and say, "See, I told you so." This is a no-win scenario.

(These are the PMs that still see themselves as successful, while their company does not.)

Here's how it works when you accept your due date as set in stone: The first thing you do is create a VIABLE plan to meet that date. You get your best, brightest, smartest talent together, and you brainstorm and research and hypothesize and make assumptions and challenge each other and thrash it out—until you arrive at a plan that all of you agree will work.

So, I accept the due date as being set in stone. I also accept my scope as being set in stone. I assume the company wants what they said they want, and I assume they have a good reason for needing it by their desired due date. But, here's the deal: I accept my resource allocation as only the fervent wish of my company. I assume my company wants to achieve the results at the lowest possible cost, and I understand their best guess of that cost is reflected in the resource allocation they first give me. Nonetheless, I am the only one who can determine what resources are needed to get the job done, and they've entrusted me to do that fairly and accurately.

PLAY WITHIN DUE-DATE BOUNDARIES

I play from the framework described above because it's the framework that puts the desires of the business first. This framework:

- Forces the most creative and brilliant solutions, simply because the constraints are so tight;
- Naturally leads to breaking the overall project work into discreet pieces, each with its own scope, timetable, and resource needs. As soon as you begin breaking the work up like this, you begin to identify those variables that add the most time, complications, and/or resources. Each of these is both a planning obstacle to overcome and a possible item to negotiate, and
- Forges very strong team bonds among your core leaders. They get to share the excitement of finding a solution to something that may at first appear impossible. They gain respect for each other's knowledge; they grow to understand their dependencies on one another, and they end up with a Big Picture of the project that will be invaluable as it moves into execution.

Good and talented people, tasked with overcoming big obstacles, rise to the challenge every time. You, the PM, will emerge from this process with a very clear Big Picture of your project, the strengths and weaknesses of your core leaders, and a glaring awareness of the main risk areas to successful delivery of your plan(s).

As you and your core co-creators thrash out all the creative ways you can achieve what your company wants from your project, you will likely surface some true project showstoppers. These are the one to five items that you and your core leaders agree *will* cause failure, and you have the evidence (often just a set of logical bullets) to back that up.

Next, you solve these showstoppers, using your three variables of time, scope, and resources. Your objective is to arrive at two or three alternative plans that are *all* viable. If any one of them is chosen, you and your team *will* be able to deliver to that plan.

Your ability to go back to your Sponsor or other executives to re-negotiate is always strongest if you can first demonstrate how the project can be done overall, highlight the showstoppers, and then lay out a recommendation for how best to overcome those obstacles. Often, they will agree to your recommendation because you have done your homework and have not backed away from their requirement.

CREATE COMPELLING ALTERNATIVES

Your project plan alternatives will be something like these:

Alternative #1
This is the one that most closely gives your company back what they gave you. It shows the given due date, scope, and resources, plus whatever extra resources you and your team may have proved are also needed. If your company chooses this alternative, they will get their scope and their due date for sure. It just may be more resource expensive than they thought. You will

need to come prepared to show that you first attempted to use only your allocated resources, but for XYZ reasons, they weren't sufficient, so you needed to add more people and/or more money.

This version is a Must-Have version. However a lot of project managers do not present it, or they don't present it in enough granularity to clearly illustrate which specific piece of the project requires more resources. They stop after proving to themselves that the variables the company initially gave them aren't viable. However, if you put yourself in the shoes of your Sponsor or your executive team, then you can see that they'll want to understand why you're asking them to give you more resources. They rarely want all the details (although YOU need to know them!), but they DO want:

- To see that you and your team put in an A+ effort in strategically and tactically thinking through all reasonable possibilities to deliver the project by the initial due date, using only allocated resources;
- To understand what, specifically, are the one to five showstoppers you uncovered during your analysis that cause you to require additional resources;
- Verification that you did appropriate and aggressive alternatives analysis, exploring all reasonable options (this is where your alternative plans come into play), and
- To understand why you need this exact number of resources, how will you use them, and where will you get them.

Alternatives #2 and #3

Each of these alternatives contains a trade-off of one or two pivotal project elements, for example:

- Reduce scope to achieve due date.
- Extend due date to avoid adding resources.
- Increase resources to achieve full scope on time.
- Extend due date and increase resources to achieve full scope.

There are endless variables in projects. You and your team need to narrow the field to the two to four strategically different alternatives that are closest to meeting the true business needs. One of these alternatives (#1 through #3) will be best. You will recommend that best alternative as the solution your company should approve and implement.

Alternative #4

Sometimes it is worthwhile to show a "Do Nothing" alternative. I present a "Do Nothing" alternative if my recommendation requires substantially more time or resources than I was given. In this alternative, I basically remind people of the project's value proposition: "Remember, if we do nothing, we will continue to lose 2% to 3% market share annually, which is a $14.5 million revenue loss over the next three years, and a drop from number two in the market to number seven." If the value proposition is substantial enough, it will still make the most sense for the business to move forward with one of your other alternatives.

This planning and alternatives analysis is common sense, and it's just good project management. It is the most strategic and important work you'll do for your company and your team, and—it's fun!

CHAPTER NINE

GET IN THE GAME OF NEGOTIATIONS

Completion of the project is not what your company wants or what they care about. What they want is to achieve a specific business goal.

You are an agent of the mission you've accepted, not the people who assigned it to you. The mission you've accepted is to design and implement the means through which a specific business goal is to be met.

PUT ON YOUR BUSINESS HAT

Let's go up to the executive level for a minute to put your project into its proper perspective. The function of projects within a company is simply to take a business decision and "make it so." Note when and how projects fit within the following executive view of the lifecycle of projects:

Who	Lifecycle of a Project, in Business Context
Business Area	• A business need is identified. • Its value proposition is quantified. (For example, "This is a federal mandate"; "This must generate $47 million in annual sales revenues.")
Governance	• The business need and value proposition are compared and evaluated against all other strategic business needs and value propositions. • A Go/No Go decision is made based on the proposition. For "Go" decisions, project resources are allocated.
Project	• The project is launched. • Throughout the project, the Sponsor and the PM keep their collective eye on the value proposition and report any risks. • *If the value proposition is severely compromised* (for example, costs are excessive, or business priorities change), then the process loops back. The business area develops a revised value proposition, which goes back into governance for a Go/No Go decision to continue the project. • The project is completed.
Business Area	• Evaluates how successfully the business need was met, calculates the actual value achieved, and reports the results to the Governance body.
Governance	• Evaluates effectiveness of their decisions, and improves decision-making processes as needed.

Here is a graphic that illustrates this same business cycle:

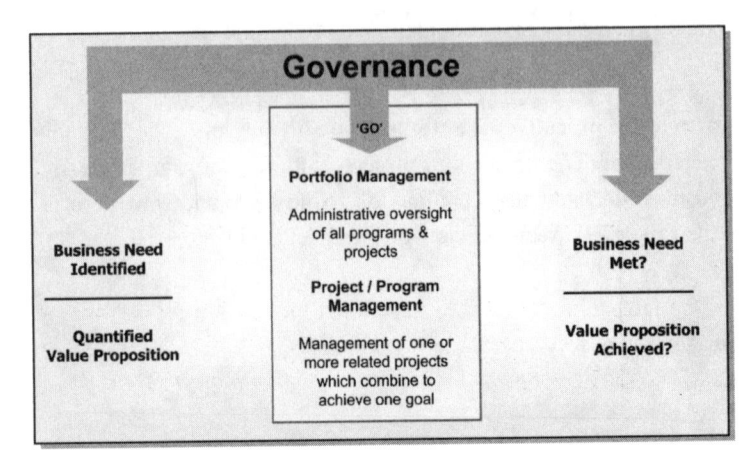

Governance

'GO'

Portfolio Management
Administrative oversight of all programs & projects

Project / Program Management
Management of one or more related projects which combine to achieve one goal

Business Need Identified

Quantified Value Proposition

Business Need Met?

Value Proposition Achieved?

Get in the Game of Negotiations

The point of the preceding chart and graph is to help you understand the whole playing field in the game of project management. If you have been thinking your role as PM is only within the 'GO' section above, then you are bypassing the full power, and the full responsibilities, of your position. In fact, the most important plays you will make occur *outside* the lines.

When you strategize, plan, think, communicate, and negotiate, your focus and language need to be on the business need and value proposition. This is your first and primary responsibility. It is also the main source of your power and authority. If you play only within the 'GO' section, you're hobbling yourself, your Sponsor, your team, and your company. Your role is bigger than that. If you don't step up to it, then everybody loses.

If you don't see it, then you can't step up to it. So, let's see what this looks like in action.

In this chapter, you'll be capturing alternative plans, assumptions, and recommendations (these were discussed in Chapter 8) in presentation format as your basis for negotiations.

If you have been operating under the kind of thinking I've been describing in these two chapters, the negotiations will be easy. Why? Because you've already integrated the thinking of the people you'll be sitting across the table from. You understand what they want to hear; you've anticipated their questions and objections; you have the sound, logical, unemotional answers prepared; you've provided viable options they can choose from; and most importantly, you are confident that you and your team have done excellent analysis and that you are presenting the best possible solution(s) for your company.

THE NEGOTIATION BRIEFING

Knowledge, preparation, and information are the most important elements you bring to the negotiating table; the briefing is how you deliver them. This negotiations briefing is one of your most important project management deliverables.

You will be evaluated, both overtly and invisibly, by more people than you will ever know, on how well you develop and deliver this briefing. You need to know this, because you need to make sure you have this broad audience in mind when you craft your briefing. Who is your broad audience?

• Your Sponsor	• Your key internal leads
• Their executives	• Key vendor leads
• Influential Stakeholders and constituents	• Your team

In most cases, you will create a basic presentation, which I call the "base deck," aimed at your Sponsor; then, you will alter it as needed to target specifically these other audiences. You want this tailoring to be slight, since you want your fundamental messages to be heard consistently by all audiences. You never know who will pass a version of your briefing to someone else, so while your emphasis may change slightly to suit each audience, you want the core briefing to be the same.

Once you've developed your base deck, typically you will craft an accompanying executive deck that you and your Sponsor will deliver to key senior executives and Stakeholders. In the rest of this chapter, I'll focus on these two briefings.

The executive deck will be much shorter and punchier. It will contain core slides from the Sponsor deck, plus an executive level summary introduction, and a call-to-action.

The content of the base deck is pretty standard. You have been given a project to do, now you're coming back to say how you are going to do it, when you'll get it done, what resources you plan to use, and how you plan to use them. As with all your briefing decks, this one will tell a story. The story here is: "This is the problem you gave us; this is what you asked us to do to solve that problem; here's what we found when we went forth to do that; now, here's how we recommend we proceed from here."

The difference between you and the PM next to you is that you will present all this information in the context of the business need and value proposition your project is designed to answer. This anchors you and your audience into the neutral and objective position of simply trying to do what's best for the business.

BRIEFING CONTENT

In the first section of the briefing, articulate your understanding of what the business community wants, why they want it, and how they'll evaluate success. In the negotiating process, this is the equivalent of you saying, "I understand this is your opening bid for a custom piece of work that you want." (Of course, you never *say* this, but all parties are aware at some level that this is true.)

The outline of this first section of the briefing looks something like this:

Possible Slide Headers...	Lifecycle of a Project, in Business Context
"Here is the business problem or opportunity."	Description of problem or opportunity, conveying magnitude, urgency, dire need
"What we need is ..."	Statement of the very high-level solution needed
"The gap is ..."	Bullets of the gaps between the current state and the desired state of the business
"So, this project was initiated to close these gaps and meet these needs."	Statement of project scope and target due date. Project objectives and targets
"Expected results are ..."	Statement of value proposition: We will expend "x" time and resources for the company's gain of "y" business benefits.

Own the Forest, Delegate the Trees

In the second section of your briefing, illustrate and explain how you plan to meet their needs and implement what they want.

Possible Slide Headers...	Related Slide Content
Project Scope	What's in / what's not
Strategy	The *thinking* parameters behind your approach
Approach	High-level description of work (bullets)
Note: Repeat the above slides for each of your two to four alternatives. (Combine information into fewer slides, if possible.) Use graphics to illustrate differences between the alternatives. Emphasize the relative costs and benefits of each item. See Chapter 8 for more information about type of content.	
Project Organization	Graphic. Emphasis on management, executive, and external roles and how they link to the project
Roles and Responsibilities	Describe management, executive, Stakeholders, advisors, and third-party roles and responsibilities. Bullet two to five responsibilities of each role. Table presentation. Possible appendix item.
Project Schedule	Graphic. Highlight phases and phase start-end dates.
Project Plan	One-page executive summary plan derived from your detailed project plan, which you'll attach as an appendix item.
Assumptions	List of pivotal assumptions for executive validation or acceptance; if these change or prove to be false, then the plan will need to change.
Call to Action	You are requesting approval of the information in this briefing, approval of the recommended solution, and agreement to the immediate allocation of resources, as requested.
Next Steps	Critical next steps (per audience). Usually involves how to go get the human resources immediately.

In the Sponsor briefing, you will lay out the full story, maybe using multiple slides to cover key points. You and your Sponsor must have a solid, shared understanding of these points, and must have a mutual agreement that the recommended solution is the best one. You are *both* accountable for turning around and helping other people understand these alternatives and your jointly recommended solution. You will likely use tailored smaller decks to most effectively connect with these subsequent audiences.

In the negotiating process, this second section is effectively either your acceptance of their opening bid or your counterproposal.

As with any contract negotiation, if the person on the other side of the table accepts your counterproposal, then you are now obligated to meet the stated terms and conditions. Your solutions in this briefing each carry your implied wet-ink signature. Each party that accepts your solution is giving an implied wet-ink signature in return.

While your company and Sponsor understand you may not be able to meet their opening bid, they absolutely expect you to meet the plan you propose back to them. So, don't ever recommend a plan, or alternate plans, unless you intend to deliver exactly what you propose.

THE BACK-AND-FORTH OF NEGOTIATIONS

So far, the two main negotiating points we've covered are:
- Wear a business hat, first and foremost, and
- Understand this is a negotiation, and craft your briefing accordingly.

Now, let's talk about the mechanics of the actual negotiations.

First, if you've done an excellent job in your briefing, you may simply get immediate approval of your recommendation. In my experience, this happens most of the time. In that second section where you've laid out possible approaches and plans, you already raised and resolved the main points that would come up in negotiation. If you think of this briefing as a form of storytelling, then you have already walked your Sponsor through the various options and their respective pros and cons. The end of the story is the inevitable conclusion that your recommendation is best.

This is not manipulative. Your company has entrusted you to find the best possible solution to a need; you did that. Now you are explaining it to someone else, showing the avenues you explored to reach your conclusion, so they can understand. *You* are not convincing them: The facts and findings that you and your team discovered during your analysis do the convincing. As a result of this analysis, you and your team have new information that your Sponsor does not. When you lay out this information, your Sponsor is highly likely to come to the same conclusions you did.

However, your Sponsor may have information you do not know. This is another key reason for you to lay out the various approaches and assumptions you explored. Your Sponsor may see where one of your pivotal assumptions is invalid. If so, that could change everything. I've seen this happen a couple of times.

In one project, I assumed business staffing practices were a given, so my solution had a long timeline for a certain business function. The Sponsor looked at that and said, "Nope, we can't afford that timeline. I will cover that business function 24/7 and have my people work in eight-hour swing shifts." His solution changed mine, and it resulted in a better answer for the company.

In another project, one of my alternatives proposed we decrease the project scope to meet a critical due date, so I proposed cutting "x" from the project. My Sponsor agreed with the need to lessen scope, but she knew that "x" was vital. She proposed cutting "y" instead. This worked just as well for the project and much better for the business.

Does it bother me that my Sponsor had a better idea? No; in fact, I love it. It tells me I'm giving my Sponsor the information needed to consider all options and select the best. It also strengthens the working bond between us, since we are both talking about strategic ways and means to get the job done. This means we both have more skin in the game.

Here is a high-level picture of what we've been talking about:

Project Negotiations

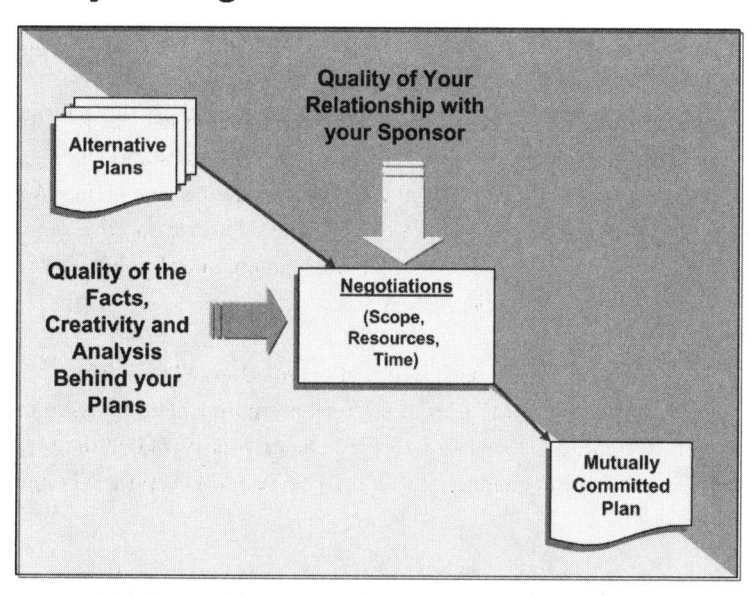

```
                    Quality of Your
                    Relationship with
                    your Sponsor
   Alternative              │
   Plans                    ▼
                    ┌──────────────┐
   Quality of the   │ Negotiations │
   Facts,           │   (Scope,    │
   Creativity and ──▶│  Resources,  │
   Analysis         │    Time)     │
   Behind your      └──────┬───────┘
   Plans                   │
                           ▼
                    ┌──────────────┐
                    │   Mutually   │
                    │  Committed   │
                    │    Plan      │
                    └──────────────┘
```

Your company and your sponsor don't want you to say 'Yes' to a plan that will fail. They want the results they expect of the project: *this is your leverage* **to get what you need to get the job done well.**

Remember when I said earlier that you will be evaluated by how well you do with your briefing and presentation? Your Sponsor is usually the person whose trust and good opinion you care about most.

In this negotiation, when you come in with solid data; you demonstrate sound analysis, business thinking, and judgment; and you present viable options for consideration, it goes a long way towards building the trust you want and need from your Sponsor.

When your Sponsor feels comfortable with you, and trusts that you are approaching and managing the project with excellence, he or she will be willing to support you as the project continues. You will get more of your Sponsor time. You will get more support and the weight of your Sponsor's influence in those times when issues arise and you need fast decisions to keep things on track.

A couple of final points regarding negotiations:

- Keep your eye on the vision, on the facts, on your experience, and on your intuition, and you will be okay.
- When you are dealing with hot items, manage and communicate facts, not emotion. Facts are your friends.
- Let other people play "The Emperor's New Clothes." It's your job to keep things real.

Section IV: Resolve Common Challenges

Overview

Your overall responsibilities as a project manager are shown in the following chart, which you may remember seeing in the introductory section. This Section IV of the book deals with the right-hand column: Resolve Ongoing Challenges.

	Project Management	
	Manage Project Lifecycle	**Resolve Ongoing Challenges**
Create, Engage and Manage Your Team	1. Clarify deliverables and targeted results 2. Plan analytical phase 3. Obtain and launch analytical resources 4. Drive viable solution alternatives 5. Prepare and negotiate alternative implementation plans 6. Obtain and launch implementation resources 7. Manage business process and technical systems design 8. Manage development and testing activities 9. Manage implementation and evaluation	Constant Crisis • Issue Resolution Process Environmental Barriers • Corporate politics, culture, and priorities • Resistance to change Relationship Glitches • People and personalities • Communication pitfalls Persistent Problems • Solution complexity • Resource constraints • Due date pressure

The "Manage Project Lifecycle" column is covered in Section VI.

In this section, IV, we will cover strategies for managing the ongoing challenges (the items on the right) that you will likely face in each of your projects. These items are not sequential work activities; they are simply things you need to deal with along the way.

You have only one management activity for *all* of these: resolve any related issues as they surface. This is an *ongoing* management activity, not a sequential one. Your strategy here as the project manager is to implement and manage an issue resolution process, which will be in play for the duration of the project.

For *each* challenge, you will be given:

- Its symptoms—what to look for, so you can catch these items early, and
- Strategic solutions—how to deal with the challenge, so you and your team can stay on track.

You will also be given an issue resolution process that, when implemented, will allow you to manage *all* of these challenges. Your job is to identify and prepare the players, to create the routine communication mechanisms, and to manage the process.

CHAPTER TEN

ACTIVATE THE ISSUE RESOLUTION PROCESS

THE BASICS

The main function of the PM, once the plan has been approved and resources allocated, is to manage those resources to the plan.

This is no challenge at all when everything is going well. But, that's never the case. If everything always went well, then you could argue that PMs would not be needed at all after the plan is developed. After all, for big projects and programs, PMs don't have any tasks on the plans; project tasks are all delegated to the appropriately skilled business and IT technicians.

Simply stated, the activity of the PM after plan approval and obtaining and assigning resources is this: Identify and remove obstacles so all assigned resources can get their jobs done. The PM must proactively, aggressively, and effectively uncover and resolve all potential problems so that the project remains on schedule. Issue resolution is not a side game; it's THE game.

124   Own the Forest, Delegate the Trees

You need to have an issue resolution process in place, and you need to lead and manage it closely. Here are the basic steps to define and implement an organized issue resolution management process:

- Identify key decision-makers and their decision accountabilities,
- Develop an issue "triage" process to flag and funnel issues to the appropriate decision-makers, and
- Implement a simple management mechanism to hold decision-makers accountable for timely resolution of their issues.

If you see any of the following symptoms in your project, then you can assume your current issue resolution process is not working well, and you need to fix it:

- Meetings established without clear purpose and direction,
- Lots of people involved in issues; it's not clear who are the decision-makers,
- No clear rules of escalation, and
- Little-to-no drive to closure.

If these above symptoms have been evident for a while, then you will likely also see:

- Chronically open issues,
- Issue churn at all levels, though mostly at lower levels,
- Enormous wasted time, at all levels, and
- Late interim deliverables, and possible project extensions.

Much of the behavior and responses of people outside your project team may not be within your designated sphere of control. You must still be able to get issues resolved in a timely manner.

Remember, you're an agent of the mission, not just the manager of a project team. The mission is bigger and more influential than you are. When it calls for timely decisions, your role is to get them, without regard to the level of the person in the organization from whom you need the decision. Your

Activate the Issue Resolution Process

authority comes from the mission. You are the one who needs to keep reminding people of the mission, so they remember its importance and they make the time to give you what is needed.

The process of issue resolution is simple:

- Project participants identify issues they can't resolve themselves (*e.g., process gaps, tool deficiencies, decision needs, resource problems, and so on*).
- They raise these issues to the appropriate party(s), per the project organization chain of command.
- These parties attend a (usually weekly) Issue Resolution meeting, in which:
- The issues get raised and logged.
- The group jointly identifies and assigns issue resolution action items and accountability to appropriate personnel.
- Assigned parties execute action items, get issues resolved, and report progress.
- Issues and action progress are routinely monitored and tracked through resolution.

Issue resolution is a group effort. As the PM, you are the facilitator of this process. You ensure specific issue resolution activities get distributed and assigned to the right people, and you routinely monitor and review issue status through resolution.

THE (AT LEAST) WEEKLY MEETING

The accountability mechanism you use to drive and enforce the issue resolution process is a simple, mandatory meeting.

The meeting needs to be mandatory, because issues come up ALL THE TIME, and if people don't have a known, immediate way to raise their issue, then they'll keep trying to work around it themselves. By the time you find out about it, it will be too late for you to direct a course of action that keeps everything on track. It's not enough to call an issue resolution meeting after someone has raised an issue. You must have a standing, at least weekly, issue resolution meeting, so you and your core leads have the chance to surface issues early and help your team address them swiftly. Ideally, you surface them when they are only *potential* issues.

You can't *personally* keep on top of all issues, but you can keep on top of the most critical ones and demonstrate to your team how seriously you take them and how quickly you get them resolved. You need to communicate to your entire project team that if they have even a suspicion that something could cause them to miss an interim deliverable due date, then they must document it and make sure it gets to you or the core lead they report to.

The agenda (below) for the issue resolution is common sense; the challenge is adhering to it. If you follow this agenda, with rigor, week after week, then it will take only about three or four meetings before your leads all understand the pattern you've established and begin to standardize what they need to do each week to prepare for the meeting. Here's how to run the meeting:

FORMAT

- You lead the meeting.
- Attendees are your core leads, plus a varying one to three other people who may be needed to explain or decide today's specific issues.
- Inputs to the meeting include the project plan and the project Issues Log (described later in this chapter).

Activate the Issue Resolution Process

FACILITATE THE AGENDA[22]

- Confirm who will be updating the document in which you'll keep track of all issues, called the Issues Log, during the meeting (it will usually be you).
- Review the status of open issues that were assigned for resolution before. This section is very brief; for example, *"Issues 4 and 7 from last week are resolved. Issue 14 is still open because we're waiting for a price proposal from the vendor. I will be getting that information from Tom by close-of-business (COB) today, and expect to have the issue resolved in our favor by COB tomorrow. The overall project timeline will not be impacted."*
- If any open issues appear problematic, then decide a solution or determination if escalation is needed, and assign it.
- Raise any new issues. Prioritize these issues, and decide which ones require immediate action.
- For each selected issue, identify and assign the best people authorized to resolve it, and the other key people who need to participate in the resolution. Then, either you or one of your core leads gets designated as the accountable party responsible for making sure assignees resolve the issue, by a designated due date.
- Close the meeting by having the issues' logger (it will usually be you) read back all open issues, and confirm assignments and due dates.

As you can see, the issue resolution meeting is a sort of triage process. Problems come into the meeting, where they get prioritized and assigned for fixing. In the next week's meeting, the fixes are reported, and new issues get tackled.

This strategy works only if you effectively communicate, manage, and monitor the entire process. If you don't keep it going and keep it effective, then it will fall apart. Issues are the rule. You must treat them as routine and common.

---

[22] This maps back to the "Rolling Agenda" tool in Chapter 18.

Communicate to your core leads that you expect them to hunt these issues out, and to report any symptoms, signs, or warnings that dates might be at risk. They need to come to each meeting able to explain the status of their assigned issues, their plans and projections if any issues are late, and a clear explanation of any new issues that have come up, including their potential impact on project deliverables or the timeline.

THE ISSUES LOG

The Issues Log is the document trail for all critical problems or barriers that surface on an ad-hoc basis throughout your project. These are work items that must get done, though they sit outside the project plan. The log itself is simple and standard. It is usually in Microsoft Excel spreadsheet format and contains the following items for each issue:

1. Issue ID Number (a unique identifier, usually a number, per issue to help people quickly find a single issue within the log)
2. Issue Type (Type often relates to pieces of work within the project, e.g., marketing tasks, training tasks, management tasks, coding tasks, and so on.)
3. Issue Status Code (O=Open, C=Closed, H=On Hold)
4. Issue Priority (H=High, M=Medium, L=Low and/or rank from 1-n)
5. Who is accountable for getting this issue resolved (the management point person for this issue)?
6. Issue Description (brief)
7. Date Issue was Opened
8. Who are the key people needed to get the issue resolved (the people with the expertise and/or decision-making authority to resolve the issue)?
9. When is the resolution due?
10. Comments/Resolution—brief bullet describing status, new information, solution
11. Date of Last Recorded Activity for Each Issue

Activate the Issue Resolution Process

SAMPLE ISSUES LOG

Sta	Issue Owner	Issues / Assumptions	Open Date	Asgn To	Due	Activities/Updates / Resolution	Last Upd
O	PM	Finance plans do not include key process steps of advance goals/obj approvals; audit trails; & milestone dates	4/1	BJ	4/30	BJ confirmed Kent has heads-up. Good meeting with Kent. Waiting for Trish's MPP plan (due 4/15) to see approval points & issues tool.	4/6
O	PM	What is Pete's acknowledged and/or hidden role re: this project? Need to obtain his dedicated time and attention & leadership & expertise immediately	4/15	Mike	4/22		
P	PM	Trish requests a template & process for addressing Deal Adds: What do we do with them, how do we get them to/from Vendor for pricing, how do we decide if in/out of contract... what to do next?	4/8	BJ	4/9	BJ spoke to Fred. Met & outlined process. Vendor template fm Sam not viable. Process drafted in PPT; 3 other-client templates found as possibilities. Waiting for Fred feedback. Then Mike/Cletis/Bob.	4/7
P	PM	In-flight projects versus all projects: general lack of clarity around project lists & sub-lists. Need to get clear internally, then decide what project info goes to Vendor, for what purpose.	4/8	Chuck	4/8	4 sub-process docs are drafted & e-mailed to Team Mgrs. Awaiting input. Then - share with Mike/Kent/Trish.	4/8
C	PM	Need 2x week scheduled mtg with Team leads	4/6	BJ	4/7	Set in Wednesday, 1st session - propose Tuesday/Thurs 4:30 or 8/9:00am. Confirmed: T/TH 8-9AM.	4/14
C	PM	Who has the definitive list of all attachments & appendices required in the contract? Who is responsible for collecting all of those documents?	4/8	Pete	4/24	vendor will provide all appendices they refer to in their SOWs. Client will provide the 3 documents required per Section 13.7(c) of the MSA: Code of Conduct; Privacy Policy; Operational Procedures Manual	4/14

Keep this log simple. It should not contain every issue ever encountered, but it must contain all issues that have the genuine potential to take the project off track, to make it exceed budget, miss deadlines, or require more resources. You need to know these things as soon as possible, so you can immediately put things in place to resolve them. You also need to decide whether to inform your Sponsor and other project Stakeholders of the threat, either as a heads-up or as an escalation step.

CHAPTER ELEVEN

KNOW CORPORATE POLITICS, CULTURE, AND PRIORITIES

It is critical that you understand the variables of politics, culture, and priorities at the very start of your project. The three of them together define the playing field on which you and your team play. If you don't understand the lay of the land, then you can't take advantage of power positions, and you can't proactively handle the pitfalls.

In my mind, you have a few choices about how to handle these variables:

- You can accept the lay of the land as it is, and strategize how to succeed with what you have;
- You can reject the lay of the land as it is, and you can try to change it as you work your project, or
- You can reject the lay of the land, ignore it, and do your own thing, or
- Any combination of the above strategies.

Looking back, I can see my strategy is almost always 90% to 95% accept things as they are and work within them strategically. The other 5% to 10% is work to change those critical few items that are so non-productive they put my project at serious risk.

I don't ignore these items. It is suicidal to do so. If ignored, then you are very likely to experience relationship issues, delays, setbacks, crisis and probable failure, any of which will make you appear ignorant. Your team deserves better than an ignorant leader, so don't be one. From Day One, make it a point to consider, analyze, and plan for the political, cultural, and priority realities you and your team face.

POLITICS

Corporate Politics is a term that describes your company's unwritten rules of engagement, specifically those that deal with how to work within the power hierarchy.

If you've been in the company for a while, you probably have already picked up these unwritten rules. It's still worth re-assessing and clarifying these at the start of each large project. Of course, if you're new to the company, or new to a specific large division or entity within the company, then you'll want to do some immediate research.

Start with the top executives. Through observation, strategic conversations, and flat-out listening to normal company gossip, understand the personal working dynamics of the top leadership team. Who is in favor with whom? Who is the generally expected successor to the CEO and/or President? Who has the most power and influence over the highest-level concerns of your project? Who is on their way out? Is there a merger in the works, and if so, what are the top leadership shake-out implications?

Then, go to the Driver tier within your project—your Stakeholders, Advisory Board members, and key constituents—and understand the same things. Absolutely understand where and how your Sponsor fits into the overall picture: The more power, influence, and good connections your Sponsor has, the luckier you are.

Your goal is to find out who has the ability to impact your project, either directly or indirectly, via their influence, relationships, and/or ambitions vis-à-vis other key people. In large projects, you will need key decisions from many of these people. The more you know about their political relationships, the faster and more smoothly you can negotiate through these relationship waters and get information to the right people, so you can get fast and effective decisions from them.

In an ideal world, you'd have the time to work up through the corporate organization structure, giving people information along the way, and persuading each of them to see the merits of whatever you are negotiating for, before you take it to the level above or next to them. In the real world, you have a tight deadline, and you'll often need a fast path to key decision-makers.

You don't want to tick off anybody along the way, and you don't want to damage relationships.

On a tactical level, this means using the "Six Degrees of Separation"[23] concept: How many relationship 'hops' does it take for you to get to the decision-maker who will give you a good decision? If either Executive 'A' or Executive 'B' could each give a good decision, and the company's hierarchical path is from you, to your Sponsor, to Executive 'A,' then *in the absence of politics*, you would follow that path.

However, if you have found out that Executive 'A' tends to say 'No' to your Sponsor's requests (perhaps because 'A' views your Sponsor as incompetent or a threat), then you could propose that you and your Sponsor approach Executive 'B' for a decision.

---

[23] In a nutshell, this concept states that any person on earth can reach any other person on earth, through six or fewer relationship links, e.g., if I wanted to reach Tom Hanks, then I could talk to my brother, who knows a screenwriter, who wrote a movie Tom acted in and met Tom on the set. (I made up this example; neither I nor my brother knows anyone who is close to Tom Hanks.)

As another example, suppose there is only one appropriate decision-maker, and that person has a serious issue with your Sponsor that could result in a poor decision. You would then seek a relationship path that puts someone else—someone who is credible and influential to the decision-maker—in front of that decision-maker. This 'someone else' would usually be a peer to your Sponsor and/or a peer to the target executive. That peer would either join your Sponsor in the meeting with the decision-maker, or attend the meeting alone and represent your Sponsor.

When you understand the political landscape, you can find a respectful and strategic path through layers of people, so you can keep your project on path and keep key people happy. When you do this, instead of triggering conflict and strife, you can deepen and strengthen relationships while moving through your fast path.

CULTURE

Corporate Culture is related to corporate politics, but it is more of a general by-product of the politics. Culture describes the common operating behaviors of people in the corporation, as they go about their work.

Again, start with the top executives, beginning with the CEO. What is their political behavior? Do they manage by consensus, by dictating, or do they partner with their expert executives on strategic decisions? Do they encourage or discourage people to work outside the strict chain of command? Do they accept negative or conflicting input, or do they want only positive agreement? Do they encourage and accept feedback, or do they discourage or ignore it? Are they creative, or stagnant? Do they make decisions quickly and stick with them, or do they make decisions slowly and then reverse them?

I'm listing strong opposites here, so the implications are obvious. Your company's leadership style sets the tone, and permeates throughout the organization. While there may be pockets within the company that seem to have their own culture—and you'll need to know if this is true—for the most part, the culture of a company is pervasive. Once you understand the culture, you can anticipate general behavior patterns, and you can devise strategies to deal with them.

If the leadership team manages by consensus,

> Then you need to anticipate that when you ask people for input and decisions, they will often be slow to give you what you need. This is because they will first want to make sure everybody and their brother agrees with them. You'll need to keep pushing for decisions and input, often through your leads. You'll need to keep reassuring people that they will not be blamed; you know some of what they provide will turn out to be incorrect, but—you need their information now anyway.

If the leadership team discourages negative feedback, or bad news,

> Then you need to anticipate that your team members will balk at giving you a heads-up of threats and risks they see. If the leadership points fingers and blames, then expect your team to do the same. The corollary behavior to this is that people won't want to step up and take visible accountability for input, actions, or decisions ... because if anything goes wrong, they know they'll be blamed for it. This behavior is very destructive to your project. Your core solution is to have an effective, proactive issue resolution process in place quickly, for the duration. You need this system to offset the personal and cultural fear people have of bringing up bad news.

If the leadership team waffles on decisions,

> Then you can expect your team to be skeptical that you'll do what you say you'll do. They will resist emotionally engaging in your project, because they won't believe it will be allowed to complete. You and your leads need to set the bar high and personally demonstrate you keep your word, you meet your own deadlines and commitments, and you succeed in all your interim deliverables—i.e., be fully prepared to lead, each step of the way.

If the leadership team engages in in-fighting,
> Then you can expect game-playing and in-fighting to take place within your constituent bodies. You'll need to know who's fighting with whom, who's winning, and who the existing peacemakers are. Your position is first to stay out of ongoing battles. You need to actively and explicitly do this; do not let yourself, your team, or your project be used as a new playground for existing hostilities. You do this by keeping your eye on the ball, and keeping all project meetings, discussions, and activities tightly focused. Your second position is to avoid or mitigate new battles caused by activities and decisions of your project.

PRIORITIES

Corporate Priorities are the relative ranking of all projects and initiatives, within the broader framework of the corporation's overall and annual mission and objectives.

This is much more obvious and tactical than the previous two items. The reason you need to know this information is, of course, because you need to know where your project falls in the mix. The higher your project is in the ranking, the more executive attention it will get, and the more readily you will get the decisions and resources you need to get and keep things on track.

A project has its own place in the corporate hierarchy. If the project calls a meeting, then it can get trumped by meetings called by higher people or projects in the corporation. You have to know where your project stands in the scheme of things, so you can prevent getting trumped, and play your project's trump card when needed.

The trick here is that people frequently play The Emperor's New Clothes: They will often keep stating that the project is a very high priority, even when it is clear the project is just one of many 'very high' priorities. If your project is only one of many very high priority projects, then this effectively means it is no higher than any of those others. People also balk from acknowledging when a project's priority level has changed mid-stream, and its importance is now less than some other urgent business need or initiative.

The impact of this 'preferred blindness' is people will continue to demand the same speed and level of project performance, at the same time they are cutting resources and brushing aside key decisions.

As the PM, you are the *objective* holder of the project torch. You are best positioned to first see these symptoms: loss of resources, and extended delays in decision-making. Because you are best positioned to see these things, it is your responsibility to make sure key decision-makers, including your Sponsor, also see what's happening, so they can re-evaluate the true priority of your project, and take appropriate action, e.g., adjust expectations, or address gaps.

Remember, you are the agent of your mission. If your project is no longer as high a priority, so what? Do not take these things personally. I see lots of PMs get upset when this happens, and it's not necessary. When priorities change, this creates another opportunity for you to be a leader for your company. It's up to you to say, "Hey—here's what's been happening on my project. It appears to be because so many of our key people are now involved in ABC effort. The impact to this project is PDQ, and the long-term impact is XYZ. I recommend we either take corrective action, or accept these implications."

When you step up to this, you help your company come to the right decisions swiftly. You also relieve your team, by either resolving the obstacles they've been seeing, or relieving them of expectations they can no longer meet.

CHAPTER TWELVE

MANAGE RESISTANCE

"There is nothing more difficult to carry out, nor more doubtful of success, nor more dangerous to handle, than to initiate a new order of things. For the reformer has enemies in all those who profit by an old order, and only lukewarm defenders in all those who would profit by a new order. This arises partly from the incredulity of mankind, who do not believe in anything new until they have had actual experience of it." — Niccolò Machiavelli

Projects implement new ideas; therefore, projects make change happen. The result of projects, especially the big ones, will result in at least some of the following changes:

- *Procedural changes*: The actual work people do, the sequence in which they do it, the speed at which they do it, and whom they work with while they do it.
- *Policy changes*: Things that were okay to do before are no longer acceptable, or extra things must be done now that never had to be done before.

- *Job changes*: Jobs get added; jobs get cut, and/or responsibilities get cut.
- *Organization changes*: Managers and executives lose their power; new people get additional power; people report to new bosses.
- *Financial changes*: Benefits, pay, bonuses.
- *Personal futures change*: The likelihood of promotion changes; the likelihood of learning new skills.
- *Relationship changes*: Communications, responsibilities, reporting, interactions, dependencies, and interdependencies.
- *Logistical changes*: Work location, office layout, tools, and equipment may change.
- *Status changes*: Any or all of the above changes can mean a status change for an individual, which means a perceived redefinition of an employee's worth to the company.

When you read this list, it's pretty clear why people resist these kinds of changes. Plus, humans tend to resist change anyway, especially when they have no input into the decision to change.

You innocently enter the project picture in the role of change agent. The actual decision-makers—the ones who approved the changes—are not visible to the people who have to change. Instead, you are the visible leader of change, so you are frequently and naturally the focal point of any resistance to it. On large projects, your key leads are often more visible than you are. Still, the resistance they will deal with also comes under your umbrella.

In order to successfully manage resistance, the first thing you need to do is to understand and accept that people resist change. Don't judge people for resisting; if you do, then re-read the list above and remember how you felt when any of these happened to you. Just accept resistance and do what you can to help people through the change.

THE WHAT AND WHO OF RESISTANCE

Change is difficult, and people's responses to it are predictable. Sometimes, it's very easy to see when someone is resisting; they might simply say, "No, I don't want that." Sometimes, people are so subtle in their resistance that they don't even know they're resisting.

Resistance comes in many forms. It's not always easy to spot, because the symptoms can be indicators of other things. Here are behavioral symptoms to look for:

- *Flat-out rejection*: "No, don't want it; won't do it."
- *Vocal criticism*: "Stupid idea; doesn't make sense; won't work."
- *Helpful advice that isn't helpful*: "This was tried before, but it failed; I told them there's a better way but nobody listens; the way you're going about it is all wrong—let me tell you how; here is a better solution; you're tackling the wrong problem—this is what you should focus on."
- *Passive resistance*: This can be the most difficult to discern. It can look like people are cooperating, when, in fact, they are digging in their heels. What you'll see is postponed meetings, late deliverables, late arrival at meetings, gossip about project or project players, slow or no decisions, slow or no deliverable reviews, slow or no response to communication attempts, and delegation of assigned tasks to subordinates (often to subordinates who don't have the knowledge or authority to move things forward).

These are things that may indicate resistance, or they may mean other things. There are times in your project where you'll solicit feedback from your team to make sure you are tackling the right issues and coming to the best solutions; the feedback your team gives you may include things on the above list. But, when these things keep coming up, unsolicited, after excellent analytic work has been completed and plans and decisions have been communicated, it's time to consider that it might be resistance.

WHAT CAN YOU DO?

The key to dealing with this kind of resistance is good communications. People need to know why the change is occurring, what benefits it will provide for the company, its customers and its employees, and what the project team is doing to help people deal with the implemented changes. It lessens their fears, and while they still may not like the facts, at least they'll know what the deal is, and that knowledge is empowering.

I recommend that for large projects, you make someone on your team the point person for general communications like these. You keep *strategic* Sponsor and executive communications responsibilities, and, through your team leads, you keep *strategic* team communication responsibilities.

For some changes, you'll need more than one person to manage general communications. For some projects, you may need to establish a PMO communications function, which publishes communications on a weekly, daily, or even hourly basis. Typically, it will do this using e-mail or voicemail broadcasts, newsletters, or bulletins; or audio/visual telecasts to one or more divisions or companies. Make sure you have a timely interactive component to these, so people can ask questions, make comments and suggestions, and get a personal response.

In addition to communicating general "what, why, and when" information, and responding to questions, there are some more specific messages which are helpful at various stages of your project's lifecycle.

Below is my own version of a Change Acceptance Curve that was introduced to me by Andersen Change Management consultants in 1995. I like it because it's focused on the project team, how they are experiencing the change, and what to do about it.

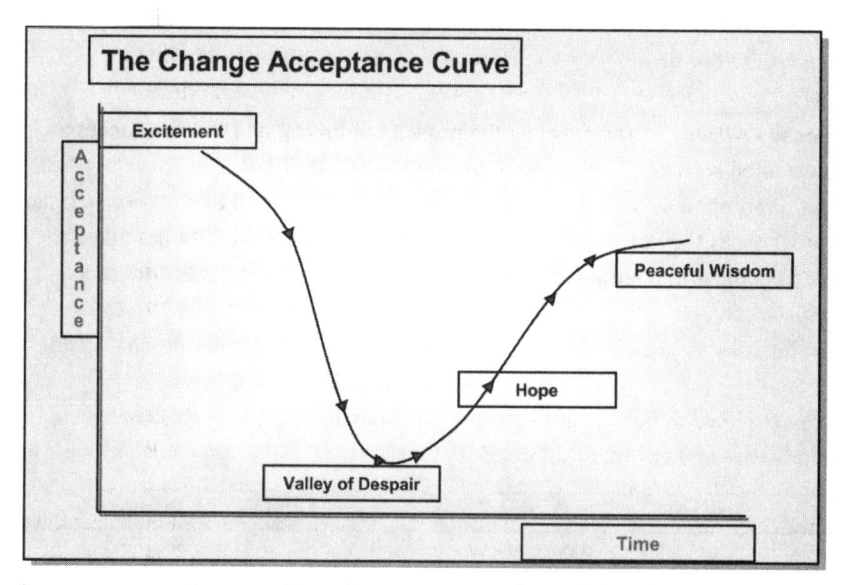

The Change Acceptance Curve

Acceptance (y-axis) vs *Time* (x-axis): Excitement → Valley of Despair → Hope → Peaceful Wisdom

As you can see, there are four phases most people go through to reach change acceptance, and they are as follows:

Phase 1: Excitement. People are excited by the upcoming change. You, the Sponsor, and the executives all start out enthused about this initiative and you spread the vision. Everyone gets revved up about the fabulous results that are certain to come as a result. Energy, enthusiasm, and acceptance are very high in this stage.

Phase 2: Valley of Despair. Very rapidly, excitement dissipates and people fall into the "Valley of Despair." This is what happens as the team looks under the covers and begins to see the enormous amount of work it will take to achieve the results. It's a kind of sticker shock. People can see the work, the problems, the long hours ahead, and all the pitfalls that could lead to failure. It feels scary, overwhelming, and disheartening, especially in comparison to the initial euphoria they experienced when the project launched.

Phase 3: Hope. As the analysis and solution design phases come to closure and people can see the light at the end of the tunnel, they start to get some energy and enthusiasm back. Even though the road to completion may still be long and hard, the work seems possible, and success seems possible. People feel on top of their piece of the project, and they understand and accept what is expected of them.

Phase 4: Peaceful Wisdom. As the project continues, and interim successes start to be seen and experienced, people's acceptance levels keep rising. Note that even upon successful project completion, people will likely not reach the initial highs they experienced when the project started. Reality has taken its toll; people are older and wiser. Still, pretty high levels are very possible.

So far, all this does is show you what to expect. Let's talk about what to do about it. The chart below shows what you can do and what you can communicate to help your team and the company handle all this change as effectively and easily as possible:

Step / Response	Need	Action / Communication
Excitement	• To care about the goal • To be excited • To receive focus and direction	You need to get people TO Excitement: • Enthusiastically and sincerely share the vision and its importance. • Share the plan, schedule, project organization chart, and make sure everyone understands their roles and responsibilities.
Valley of Despair	• To believe success is possible • To believe they can deliver what's being asked of them	You need to get people OUT of the Valley of Despair: • Remain ahead of the game. • Quickly get plans to detail levels 2 & 3. • Be confident in your plans, and project certainty of success continuously. • Implement and enforce routine meetings and communications. • Implement and closely manage an issue resolution mechanism. • Re-clarify roles and responsibilities. • Celebrate small victories.

Hope	• Motivation to stick with it	You need to help people stay energized for the duration: • Keep celebrating interim successes. Demonstrate the behavior you want: Meet your deadlines, communicate timely and effectively, do what you say you'll do, when you say you'll do it. • Manage people to the plan. Let them know you're on top of it; you're holding people accountable for their tasks and deliverables (*see Chapter 17 "Manage Due-Date Pressure"*). • Remove barriers for your team. Get rapid decisions from Sponsor, executives, and Stakeholders when needed.
Peaceful Wisdom	• To feel successful • To feel appreciated and valued (People need these all along, of course.)	You need to honor the people who created this success for the business: • Celebrate success. • Acknowledge individual contribution, and do it personally. • Ideally, acknowledge individual contribution publicly and financially.

Consider this outline to be an ideal to strive for; you may never be able to fulfill all of these needs, as fully as described in this chart.

The fact is that you will have excellent people on your team who have very high degrees of integrity and pride in their work. They will produce excellent work despite you if they have to; that's just who they are. So, if you don't do all these things, then your project can still be successful. These are the things that can help make you an excellent leader in life, so it's always worthwhile to do as much of these as you can.

---

[24] Examples of simple interim celebrations include: take team to lunch; hold "teammate of the month" celebration with peer votes for recognition and awards; congratulate individuals for achieving key milestones (verbally and/or in a note); post success stories in company, division, and/or department newsletter (make sure to list names of stellar contributors).

Two last thoughts as you work with people who are knowingly or subconsciously resisting change:

- People have hot buttons. Don't push them.
- You have hot buttons. Know what they are, and manage them.

RESISTANCE TO CHANGE WITHIN YOUR TEAM

As covered above, resistance to change is evident when people put up obstacles to your project's success. They do this consciously and unconsciously. I believe what is going on here is largely fear.[25] Fear of the unknown, fear of loss of income, loss of status, loss of control, and loss of friends and relationships. What may also be going on is resentment: "I could do that better; my idea is better; I'll just be working myself out of a job; this will take a lot more hours and I'm just not putting in any more; I've gotten excited about projects before, but they've failed and I'm just too tired (burnt out, cynical, wise) to get all excited about this one."

If a person feels these fears or resentments, then resistance is a logical response.

As the PM, your proactive response to their *fear* is to provide timely and factual information:

As soon as people have reliable facts, even if they don't like them, they know what they face and they feel more in control. Also, most fear is ungrounded, and comes from people's imagined worse-case scenarios, often fed by gossip and rumor. As soon as you give them information they can trust, much of their fear goes away because they can see the worse-case scenario is not real. Even when the worse-case scenario does come true, such as cutting jobs, there is relief and empowerment in knowing for certain.

---

[25] I am not a psychologist; I have no formal training, degree, or certification in psychology or the analysis of people and personalities.

I generally start my communications by using the approved Sponsor briefing as my information source. I, or someone on my team, cut and dice it to customize it for different audiences; then, we deliver that information or assign the delivery of that information. A key message in each of these communications is the "Next Steps" slide or bullets. This is where you think through the probable specific concerns of your audience (ideally, you have asked them for their concerns first); then, either let people know the answers or give them a date by which you will have answers for them.

How to deal with people's *resentment* is not as obvious.

My approach is to avoid getting tangled up in the fear and resentment my project may stir up, and instead I hit the ground running. I work hard and rapidly to get momentum rolling, establish roles and responsibilities, and engage people in beginning their work. I share my vision, passion, and commitment for the project mission to help instill a sense of urgency and just generally get things moving. In this way, we very quickly come upon and meet our initial due dates and that delivers an important message: This baby's moving; it will be successful, so jump on board or get out of the way.

This approach sets the stage for success and lets team members share the benefits of that success. Success has a very different energy and appearance than failure or than just going through the motions. People like to be part of something that will succeed; it's exciting, energizing, invigorating, and challenging. People perceive the real possibility that they could end the project feeling good about what they've done.

The possibility of feeling really good about the work you do is very rare in some companies. If your project offers that possibility, then many people might be moved to choose to give you and your team a chance by stepping up to full participation and becoming a willing, vital part of the team.

CHAPTER THIRTEEN

PAY ATTENTION TO PEOPLE AND PERSONALITIES

Successful project management is two-thirds about establishing, sustaining, and growing effective working relationships and one-third about understanding and applying basic processes and structure. If you don't know how to effectively engage people in the work of your project, then you will likely have a short career in this field and/or a painful one.

Own the Forest, Delegate the Trees focuses a lot on the relationship aspect of project management, and on how project relationships look and act within key project activities and processes. In most cases, these relationships are described in terms of specific roles and how those roles engage and interact.

In this chapter, the focus is on people and personalities in general, regardless of role. Each of us carries a certain set of assumptions and beliefs about people, and those assumptions and beliefs flavor and, in some cases, determine how we interact with others.

This chapter describes assumptions and beliefs that tend to create successful and effective interactions and relationships. You'll see examples of how these assumptions and beliefs play out in a project environment.

PEOPLE

Here are recommended people assumptions about anyone you work with:
- People are basically good.
- They want to be successful.
- They want to be respected.
- They want to feel important.
- They want to be heard.
- They want your project (their project!) to be successful.
- They will help if they can.
- They will do their job well, as long as they know what their job is.
- They will make the right decision, if you present the relevant facts to them, in a clear and logical manner.
- You are the project and program management expert; they are the expert in their particular field.

If I am ever having difficulty with a person, I can usually look at my own words and actions with them, and find I've overlooked or disregarded one or more of these assumptions. If one of my leads is having people problems, I can usually find they've overlooked or disregarded the same.

If I have people difficulties on my team, I know two things: 1) I've helped create that difficulty, most likely by ignoring one of the above-listed assumptions, and 2) If it needs to be resolved, then it's my responsibility to resolve it.

Before I resolve it, however, I have to first prioritize the problem. I have to decide whether this particular people-problem is worth resolving, or if it's one we both just need to live with.

The fact of the matter is, when you are the head of a very large program or project, you are in an active working relationship with, minimally, all the people who are named in your project plans and/or in your project

Pay Attention to People and Personalities

organization chart. You probably interact with at least twice that many people on a monthly basis. A lowball estimate of the number of people with whom you might have personal contact each week on large projects is 100.

If you have some kind of people-problem with one of those 100 people—for example, someone is upset because you didn't get their input on a decision you made—you have to think about whether their being upset is a threat to your project. How upset are they? Are they a key Stakeholder? Are they likely to try to put obstacles in your way? Do they have the power and influence to put obstacles in your way? Are they a long-term player on the project?

It's impossible to draw a line in the sand to say which people issues should be actively addressed, and which are best left alone. Here's a rule of thumb anyway: If the people-problem involves one of your key leads, or your Sponsor, or a Stakeholder, or an executive, then you absolutely must resolve it. If it's anyone you see regularly, then you must resolve it. If it's quick and easy to resolve, then resolve it.

My guess is that every single day I make decisions on my projects that upset somebody. Also, as the head of my project, I am often on the front line as the communicator of decisions *other* people have made ... these decisions can upset people, who get upset with me as the bearer of that bad news. If I were to get upset right back about each and every single one of them, I'd never get anything done. If I were even to *respond* to each and every single one, I'd lose the ability to do my job and keep the whole team focused forward.

So, in many cases, I just allow people to be upset on their own, and I trust they will deal with it themselves. Usually, the situation is very temporary: Someone is miffed when they first hear about something, but then they're okay with it 24 hours later. Remember the assumption list: People are basically good; they want the project to be successful; they will help if they can. For these reasons, when people get miffed (usually because I haven't done an excellent job with the other assumptions that might make them feel heard, respected, important, and informed), they will get over it, usually by looking at the bigger picture themselves to see no harm or disrespect was intended.

When I go to resolve a people issue, as I said earlier, I consider my assumption list. When I see an assumption I've overlooked or disregarded with this person, my solution will be to acknowledge my oversight, and to address that assumption now.

It's pretty simple human dynamics. The only trick is owning up to your part in creating the current problem, letting go of whatever blaming you may be tempted to do, and choosing to be responsible for your own actions by correcting them. It looks like this:

If I fail to honor this assumption ...	Then I must now show this person that ...
People are basically good.	• I trust they are a good person.
They want to be successful.	• I see them as successful.
They want to be respected.	• I respect them.
They want to feel important.	• I believe they are important.
They want to be heard.	• I have heard them (repeat back), or • I am ready to hear them now, or • I wish I could have heard them (but XYZ prevented it), or • I commit to consult with them on similar points in the future. (Note: People will usually want this one, but it's often not possible for you to commit to it. Be careful.)
They want my project to be successful.	• I know their intentions are good and that they are trying to help.
They will help if they can.	• I know they are trying to help, • Here, precisely, is how I need them to help, and • I understand the other responsibilities they have which makes it difficult, perhaps impossible, for them to help me as I need, and • I offer my support in showing how much my project needs them, so they can be freed to do so if possible.

Pay Attention to People and Personalities

They will do their job well, as long as they know what their job is.	• I am confident they will do the job well. • I (or one of my leads) will make the time to help this person get a full and complete understanding of their roles, responsibilities, assignments, due dates, and deliverables.
They will make the right decision, if I present the relevant facts to them, in a clear and logical manner.	• I must present the relevant facts to them, in a clear and logical manner. • I must listen to any new information they may share, which must be considered to reach the right decision for the company.
I am the project and program management expert.	• I must acknowledge where I may have assumed they knew things, e.g., their roles and responsibilities, the urgency of their task or decision, when it was my accountability to inform them, ensure they understand, remind them, and track their progress.
They are the expert in their particular field.	• I must acknowledge that they have information, facts, and expertise I and my team do not, and that we are responsible for soliciting it from this person in a timely and effective manner.

A few points about this table:

Just because it contains the word 'I' does not mean you, personally, need to do this action. Remember, *own the forest, delegate the trees*. Use your judgment—in some cases, it is imperative that you do personally show up and resolve the issues. Certainly if you actively caused some specific problem, then you must actively resolve it.

In many cases, however, people issues will be directed to you as the leader, but they can be resolved by other people on your team through information- and fact-sharing. I delegate as many of these as I can to other people. To show my respect and to complete the circle, I do let the concerned individual know I am responding to them via this other person. I do this in person, via voice or e-mail, or simply by telling my delegate to let the person know that "Barb sent me to you to address your concern."

The above list of possible action items is by no means conclusive.

The key word in the header of this action column is 'Show.' You don't need to necessarily *say* "I respect you"—though it never hurts, as long as you're sincere. You do need to *show* the other person you respect them by the quality and content of your response: If an apology is in order, then make one. If an explanation is in order, then give it. If information is needed, then provide it. If a change in process or communications is needed, then propose it.

PERSONALITIES

In my experience, people tend towards one of four personality types. The following table describes each personality type, and lists behavioral clues you can look for in people to help you identify which type they may be:

Type	Description	Behavior Clues
Bottom-Liners	These are the people who want you to get right to the point, but be able to back up that point with great data.	*Bottom-Liners* say, "Get to the point." They skim ahead through your briefing while you're still covering the table of contents. They check their watch frequently. They shift in their seat or roll their eyes while you talk. They break in and ask, "So, what's the bottom line?"
Analysts	These are the people who want to know all the answers, the whys, and the hows. They are not very comfortable with estimates or guessing; they want to know and understand.	*Analysts* ask lots of questions, specifically Why and How. They jump right to the obstacles in most brainstorming and discussion sessions. They want details and specifics. They are impatient with concepts, and want to move right into doing something.

Creatives	These are the people who can't be bothered by facts, though they like to know facts are hanging around. They prefer oral and visual communications, and resist things like tasks lists and structure.	*Creatives* are friendly, outgoing, and get excited moving from idea to idea. They often leap from topic to topic in their speech, without feeling the need to close any along the way. They'd rather not be bothered by pesky details such as how to get the thing done. They tend to be very engaging and energizing.
Socials	These are people who enjoy and expect the social pleasantries of communications. They like to connect personally before delving into business. They like the story, not just the ending. They often like form as much as content.	*Socials* are also friendly, but more so; they are most comfortable and at ease when people follow generally accepted social and professional protocols. They appreciate a step-by-step approach, and will work steadily within such an approach.

The best way to connect with a person is to adapt to their personality type for your interactions. Another word for this is empathy. You are simply discovering their interaction preferences, and choosing theirs over your own.

Adapting your style is easier said than done. I'm a Bottom-Liner, and it can be a challenge for me to even think about these considerations ... because I'm already at the bottom line. I'm sure it's a challenge for everyone, no matter which is their most dominant type, to remember to bend first towards the preferences of the other person. As a fellow human being, it's the most caring and considerate approach. As a professional, it's also the most effective. As the PM, it may be essential to your project's success.

TIPS FOR WORKING WITH EACH PERSONALITY TYPE

Bottom-Liners: Don't make them wait for the bottom line; give it to them immediately. Then, be prepared to back it up with a few summary bullets, if asked. If you are looking for them to make a decision or take some other action, say so right up front, and then be able to clearly and concisely explain what you need and why you need it. Speak and write in short, bullet sentences—never ramble on. Know your stuff, and be able to answer questions if asked.

Analysts: Acknowledge their desire for facts. Give facts and details whenever you can. Put them in writing—even better. Acknowledge when you don't have answers to their questions, or facts to give them. When asking for immediate answers or input from them, make a point of assuring them that you understand their input is based on many assumptions and best-guesses, and that their feet will not be nailed to the wall if their answers turn out to be off.

Creatives: If you are not already at their energy level, then kick yourself up a notch. Be excited and enthusiastic with them, and then lead them gently but firmly to the questions or decisions you need from them, e.g., "That's a great idea! Let's brainstorm for a couple of minutes about how we can make that happen." Brainstorming is fun for Creatives; analysis and detailed design are painful and difficult. Don't expect tactical, operational, step-by-step thinking to initiate from these people. They respond well, and provide great input, when presented with a first draft of something. When you meet with them, walk in with lists, pictures, any written thing to show them. Ask them to confirm or correct these things with you, and capture their input.

Socials: Honor their preferences and take the time to greet them and chitchat for a couple of minutes, perform introductions if other people are present, give people time to settle into their seats, and then lay out the meeting purpose and agenda. This time and structure is important to Socials. Think of it as you being the meeting host or hostess; all they want from you is to first treat them as guests and ensure they are at ease before you dive into work.

Pay Attention to People and Personalities

It is well worth your time to make the effort to tailor your communications for the other person. When you keep the other person's interaction preferences in mind, it's very easy to relate to them comfortably, and to speak to them in a way that's efficient, effective, and yields the results you want.

YOUR PERSONAL LEADERSHIP

You are human. More than likely, you are not always the leader you wish yourself to be. Your leadership gaps and flaws can become pretty obvious when leading a project because you have so many new relationships and so little time to develop them. You also have large accountabilities and tight, tight deadlines. Whatever "buttons" you have, in a project environment, people *will* push them.

So, what to do?

First, let me say there are better resources than me to answer this question. My favorites are:

- *The Success Principles* by Jack Canfield, published by Harper Collins Publisher, Inc. This is such a solid, rich resource I recommend you keep it on your desk for immediate ideas, and for reminders whenever you need them. It's written so you can get great value from reading even a two- to three-page section.

- Anything by Ken Blanchard. My personal favorite is *The One Minute Manager Meets the Monkey*, published by William Morrow & Company (January 1991) from Harper Collins Publisher, Inc. (December 28, 2004), which is focused on identifying what and how to delegate. Dr. Blanchard's books are short, easy to read, and he keeps things simple and usable.

My two cents on top of these masters?

First, know your personal leadership strengths and weaknesses. This doesn't have to be a big deal. If you want to get clarity on this, I recommend this simple exercise:

> Sit down in front of a blank sheet of paper, create the column headings 'My Strengths' and 'My Weaknesses,' set a timer for 15 minutes, and spend the entire 15 minutes adding items to each column. (If you get stuck, you can Google on the keywords 'leadership traits' for ideas.) When the 15 minutes are up, spend one extra minute and circle the top three items in each column, representing your greatest strengths and greatest weaknesses.

Once you know your top three strengths, write them in a private place where you will still see them often. Whenever you are in a difficult or crisis situation, remember you are very strong in these three areas; choose to lead with one of them.

Here's an example of how this works:

You are sitting in a meeting with eight other people. An issue was raised 10 minutes ago; everyone is hot and bothered about it, and the conversation is circling around but getting nowhere. You are not the leader of the meeting, but you are the leader of the related project.

You need to act, so this meeting gets productive. Let's say your strengths are your respect for others, your analytical skills, and your sense of humor. Since you need to be immediately effective, you will rely on your strengths. You now have a specific focus for finding a way to turn this meeting around: Focus on your three strengths. Your thoughts could flow something like this:

- *Respect:* "Everybody's talking and no one is listening; it would be helpful if I could provide each person with the respect of being heard."
- *Sense of Humor*: "I could crack a joke, or look for some humor in what's going on … hmm, nothing funny is coming to my mind."

Pay Attention to People and Personalities

- *Analytical Skills*: "This has gotten too emotional; it would be helpful if I could help people look at this topic objectively."

You choose your respect for others and your analytical skills, and you walk to the whiteboard and say something like "I've been hearing lots of different points here; let's capture them and see what the picture really looks like. We can move from there and figure out what to do about it." I show respect by volunteering to write down people's points, and by drawing everyone's eye to the board, I begin to move them to a more objective, analytical way of looking at the issue.

That's an example of using your strengths. For your areas of weakness, I recommend you find people who are strong in those areas, and rely on them to close those gaps for you.

Here's an example of this:

One of my weaknesses is that I can be too left-brained (analytical, fact-oriented, objective) when I write and when I speak. When this happens, I focus only on the facts of a situation, and lose sight of the feelings of the people in the situation. In most cases, being left-brained is a strength. But, in certain communications and situations being too left-brained can damage relationships.

When I recognize I'm in a volatile situation, or that I'm dealing with volatile people, I select more right-brained (creative, feeling, expressive) people on my team to preview my notes and papers, or listen to my planned presentations. I ask them if my tone is okay, and if I am phrasing and presenting things in a way that will be well received by my audience. I tweak whatever their feedback tells me to tweak. This strategy has worked very well for me.

Of course, another option for handling weaknesses is to become strong in your weak areas, but this can take time. On a project, you have to pick and choose the best use of your time. Using other people's strengths where you are weak is an effective solution.

Some last thoughts on this topic:

- Do the best you can with the skills and strengths you have, and forgive yourself when you screw up.
- Recognize that as the leader, you will not be beloved by everyone. People will disagree with you, your methods, and the project objectives. Accept this, and don't let it throw you.
- Focus on improving no more than one to three of your personal leadership traits in any one project; otherwise, your evolving behaviors will confuse yourself and your team.
- Don't let personal conflicts simmer. Have the courage to admit errors and apologize when you know it's the right thing to do.

CHAPTER FOURTEEN

BE A COMPELLING COMMUNICATOR

Communications is the only tool you have that lets you bridge the gap between what you see and believe about your projects, and what your constituents see and believe. *The absolute most important success structure you must put in place up front is the project communications structure.*

This next chart shows that the skill of communication becomes more and more important the higher you move up the management chain. What it also shows is that once you become a more senior manager, the bulk of your time is spent in communications activities versus technical activities.

Communications is a topic that most of us understand is critical, yet it too often gets kicked aside as an "I'll get to that later" item.

If you do not make strategic project communications a key, routine part of your day-to-day job as PM, then you will not be successful on projects that are visible and important to your company. These are the projects you want to lead. These are the ones where you get to showcase your talents and earn more money, promotions, and prestige. These are the ones that are easier to get resources for and easier to get executive involvement and commitment.

Project Management Skills Mix

▓ Communication & People Management Skills
☐ Technical or Business Process Skills & Know-How

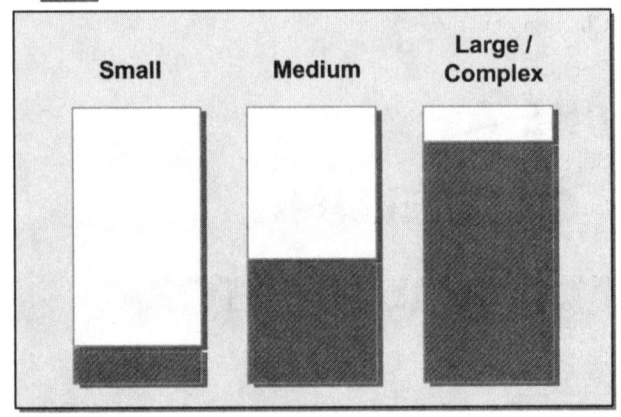

| Small | Medium | Large / Complex |

As your projects get bigger and more complex, your communication & people management skills become far more important than your technical or business know-how.

YOU ARE THE COMMUNICATIONS HUB

You are the communications hub for your project. Literally, all core information—vision, mission, strategy, ideas, plans, schedules, roles and responsibilities, status, issues, projections, changes, tasking, etc.—flows to and from you.

One thing the preceding chart does not tell you is whom you communicate with. In my experience, as your projects get bigger, more complex, more urgent, and more visible, your communication focus will shift from downward into your team to a more upward and outward audience. The bigger things get, the more you need to focus on your Sponsor, Stakeholders, advisors, and executives, and the less you can personally afford to focus on your SMEs and developers. This is because the bigger your project gets, the more it is susceptible to external as well as internal events.

Examples of external events that could impact your project include:
- Market fluctuations
- Economic shifts
- Changing customer needs
- Regulatory changes
- Changes in competitor make-up or behavior
- Supplier policy or pricing changes
- Emerging company priorities

You cannot usually influence these things, but you can 'project manage' around them. You need to see these things in advance and head them off at the pass before they block your team. In many companies, this takes a lot of education and relationship building. This takes time and energy to identify and manage the specific corporate support and actions needed to enable your project.

Since you must devote an extra degree of time to communicating upward and outward, that means you must delegate some of your project management accountability for communicating downward. You must *delegate* because you can't afford to *cut back* on your downward communications; your team needs to know your vision, objectives, plans, their role, their deliverables and timetables, or they can't perform.

So, how do you still achieve appropriate communications to your team while spending extra time with your other constituents? You do this via your masterminds [*see Chapter 6*] and/or delegation to your key leads or subordinate PMs. At some point, you may need extra resources to handle these extra communications. Usually, this is where you need another PM, who will pick up these communications as part of his or her role.

FAULTY COMMUNICATIONS IS THE ROOT OF MOST PROBLEMS

When something is going wrong with your project, the most likely root cause will turn out to be a communications issue.

In the table that follows, the first column (A) lists some examples of things that go wrong on projects; the second column (B) shows the problems that likely led to those things; and the third column (C) shows communications gaps that could be the root causes of the problems. Since you are the communications hub of the project, this third column presents you as the responsible party:

(A) Facts of the Situation	(B) Likely Problems	(C) Possible Root Cause / Project Management Gap
Someone's expectations are unrealistic.	• They do not understand the facts.	• You have not effectively presented the facts in a logical and conclusive manner. • You do not have a mutually agreed upon plan.
Someone's work is late.	• They did not commit to meet that date, • Did not know the date, • Did not understand the task, or • Did not know or trust the person to whom they should have escalated whatever issue was in the way.	• You did not gain their commitment to their tasks and due dates. • You did not clarify the task and/or adequately describe the required deliverable. • You do not have an effective issue resolution process in place so people can proactively raise issues to those who can resolve them.

Be a Compelling Communicator

Someone is not making timely decisions.	• They do not understand the factual costs of the delay, • Don't understand their role, • Don't have or understand the information they need to make a decision, or • Did not know and commit to a due date.	• You did not find out and then provide the information they need to make a decision. • You did not coordinate their time to receive the information, review it, discuss it, and render a decision. • You did not successfully get their time commitment to make this decision.

The fact that you are *responsible* for these things does not necessarily mean you are responsible for personally *doing* these things. Many times, yes. But, especially on large projects, it's often appropriate to delegate these communications tasks to others on your teams. You do remain accountable that these kinds of communications are occurring routinely and effectively within your teams.

As the PM, it's important you see these kinds of situations clearly. Too many times, PMs just look at the items in the left column above and blame that person. Or, they see the items in the second column, but still blame the other person; for example, "I *told* Bob that getting this done in three months was unrealistic!" The best PMs—the best leaders—live in column (C) and ask themselves "What do I need to do to resolve or prevent items from getting into column (A)?"

For example, if you had told Bob that a timeframe of three months was unrealistic, but Bob is still expecting the job to be done in three months, then you have not been successful in showing him the facts as you see them. Or, he knows facts that you don't know. In any case, at least *one* of you does not have the full story, and it is preventing you from achieving a mutually agreed upon plan.

All this being said, there are some people who will not ever 'get it.' If you are dealing with one of these people, then what might be needed is a workaround. Who else in the organization has the authority to make the decision you need, or has the expertise you need to solve a problem? If you can't prevent or resolve issues with person 'x,' then you need to identify and work with a backup.

For the purposes of this chapter, just understand the root cause of most issues that surface in your project are *not* due to specific people, e.g., "My Sponsor is an idiot." The root cause is *usually* ineffective communications.

If it were true that the problem is the person, then this would be blaming, and it would leave you with your hands tied. But, since the problem is communications, this is your responsibility, and it leaves you with options and opportunity.

PROJECT COMMUNICATIONS BASICS

Here is a graphic that shows the types of communications information that need to be managed in a typical project:

Project Communications Content

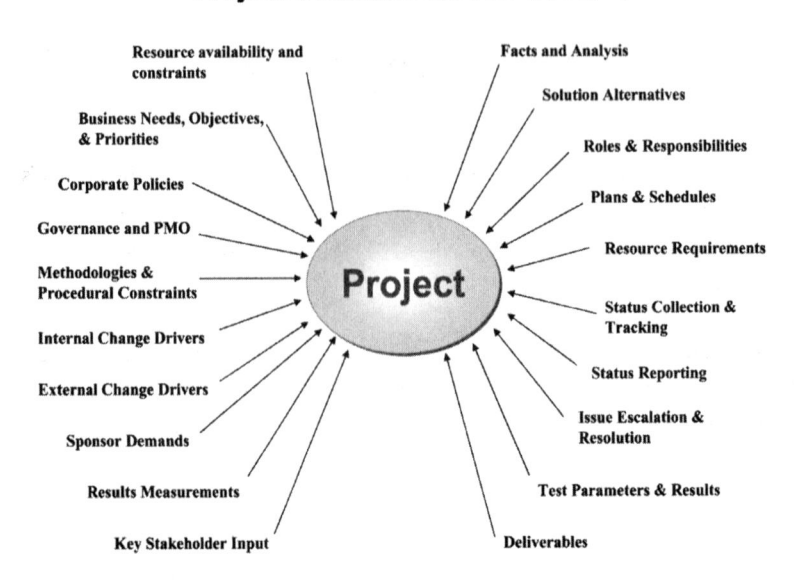

Inputs to Project:
- Resource availability and constraints
- Business Needs, Objectives, & Priorities
- Corporate Policies
- Governance and PMO
- Methodologies & Procedural Constraints
- Internal Change Drivers
- External Change Drivers
- Sponsor Demands
- Results Measurements
- Key Stakeholder Input

Outputs from Project:
- Facts and Analysis
- Solution Alternatives
- Roles & Responsibilities
- Plans & Schedules
- Resource Requirements
- Status Collection & Tracking
- Status Reporting
- Issue Escalation & Resolution
- Test Parameters & Results
- Deliverables

You have two goals with communications. The first is to get a fast and accurate initial understanding of input opportunities and constraints. The second is to establish ongoing, two-way communication mechanisms, so you can:

- Find out immediately if a significant change occurs in any of these areas that could impact your project, and
- Keep all constituents appropriately informed, so they can manage their resources to meet fluctuations in project plans and keep all their constituents appropriately informed.

It's your ongoing job to protect your team from Big Feet stomping on your project from above. It's your ongoing job to protect your Sponsor and key Stakeholders from unpleasant surprises coming out of left field. Building and honoring an excellent communications infrastructure in your project is the way you accomplish both.

You want happy, informed, and comfortable people above you. So, anticipate and answer their questions before they need to ask. This keeps them in the loop (which they like and need), which means they remain calm and stay out of your hair (which you like and need). Be reliable, proactive, respectful, and accurate in your communications, and you will do fine.

SHARING PROBLEMS

Generally speaking, you share problems because you need somebody else's help to resolve them. If you can fix it yourself, then don't bother others. It doesn't win you any points, and may cause others to panic and begin stomping all over your project.

When reporting a problem, one thing you can count on is triggering some degree of fear of failure in your audience. Here are some 'Consequence' statements that mobilize people to action by connecting with their fear:

Event	Call to Action	Consequence of Inaction
Reviewers missed their due date.	Reviewers must provide their input no later than noon xx/xx/xx.	If reviewers don't provide input by noon xx/xx/xx, we have two choices: a. Proceed without their input, which means we'll have an estimated 30% reduction in quality, or b. Accept and integrate the input later, which means re-work, which means we'll miss the project due date. We'll default to (a).
SMEs are missing meetings.	Finance department must free SME resources to attend project meetings as their top priority, immediately, for the next three weeks.	Finance SMEs missed 50% of scheduled meetings. This is a direct hit to the timeline. Unless we get SME attendance to 100% immediately, this project will not meet its targeted due date.
System crashed.	Heads up: The XYZ project implementation is negatively impacting us.	System has crashed twice this week, so we've lost two test cycles. We have managed around this so far, but if it keeps occurring, it is a threat to our due date.
Architecture we need is not in compliance with standards.	Executive decision needed.	Red Flag. The architecture design we planned is out of compliance. The in compliance solution will add three months to the timeline and $1.2 million to costs. Requires governance decision. Project is stalled pending decision.

Three notes before leaving this section:

1. As you do this kind of pre-communications strategic thinking, it becomes easy and natural.
2. Before you put any problem information in a written status report, make sure that you first made this exact information clear to the particular person who needs to act. Give them the chance, and the courtesy, of clearing the problem. Ideally, very few issues rise to your status report because you've brought them to the right people in time for them to take remedial action.
3. If you are introducing massive change, then you will need a much more sophisticated communications model than I am showing here. Establishing and staffing this more sophisticated model would be an action item, and possibly a sub-project, in your overall project plan; for example, "Develop, implement, and manage the project communications system."

YOUR PERSONAL DEVELOPMENT

Though I touched on this in the previous chapter, it bears repeating here in this chapter on communications. As a leader of people, the most beneficial ongoing learning you can do is to work on your people skills. The core of your relationship skills comes from your relationship with yourself. You need to be aware of not just your technical, project management skills and abilities, but you also need to be aware of your strengths and weaknesses in connecting with, influencing, inspiring, and leading people.

As you move higher and higher up in the leadership ranks, your success is based more on your communications skills, and less and less on your technical skills.

If you first came to be a PM because you were a technical expert, for example, in IT, manufacturing, or business process systems, you cannot afford to cling to that expertise once you are the PM of a large project. Your team does not need your technical expertise; they need someone who has project management, leadership, communications, and relationship expertise.

No matter how successful I already am as a PM and as a leader, I always have plenty of room to grow in these areas. I set personal growth goals for myself at the start of each project, e.g., to learn to work effectively with one of the personality types; to lead as a service to my Sponsor, key constituents, and team leads; to demonstrate energy and commitment, etcetera.

You may want to do a self-assessment to see if there is a particular skill or set of skills you'd like to develop. Here is a set of questions you could ask yourself:

1. Do you connect easily and well with people?
2. Are you generally well respected?
3. Do you lead by example?
4. Do you say what you mean and mean what you say?
5. Do people trust you?
6. Do you inspire people?
7. Do people rise to new levels of performance when they work for you?
8. Do people generally know what you want them to do, and do they deliver what you need them to deliver?
9. Do you have the reputation you want?
10. Do you attract great people to work with you?

If you identify a skill you want to grow or develop, brainstorm a list of 10 or so actions you could take within the scope of your current project to grow and practice those skills. Select three of those 10 possible actions, and—that's your personal development plan.

You can find other recommendations for personal and leadership development books and training programs on my website: *www.ProjectLeadershipGold.com.*

I've given you short and simple guidelines in these last two chapters, because I know how little time you have in each project to create and develop the comfortable, effective, and fun relationships you want and need.

In my life, I've mastered the 'effectively' and 'productively' aspects, but I have stumbled from time to time within the 'respectfully' and 'peacefully' areas. As a human being, I'd prefer to have this the other way around. I rarely question my pure professional decisions after-the-fact, but I have questioned *how* I've chosen to handle certain interactions. It's this human stuff that has kept me up nights: "Did I treat that person with empathy and respect, in a way I would like to be treated?" It hurts them if I haven't (I'm not talking primarily about emotional pain here); it hurts me, and it takes time to address and resolve.

Learning to deal well with people is one of the most valuable personal and professional skills you can master. I encourage you to do so. Graceful relationships are a source of great joy and peace.

CHAPTER FIFTEEN

BELIEVE SOLUTIONS ARE POSSIBLE

Solution complexity can include many elements, for example:
- Needing a solution that crosses departmental, divisional, or even company organizational and functional lines;
- Needing a far bigger solution than you have time or money to work with;
- Having a very large team to manage;
- Having a diverse team comprising many different skills and experience levels, and possibly different languages;
- Having a geographically spread team;
- Having external consultants, vendors, clients, and/or advisory boards on your team;
- Having company technical or other standards that may not be economically appropriate for your project, and so on.

I can't offer you specific advice here to deal with all of the possible complexities you will face on your project. What I can tell you is: A solution is always possible, as long as you believe it is.

I've never run across a project, whose solution—either solving a problem or creating a possibility—could not be discovered and created by my teams and me. Not all our solutions have been elegant and pretty ... but they've met the business need, within the negotiated scope, schedule, and budget.

The phase of the project where we get to 'figure it all out' is my absolute favorite. I get to be surrounded by incredibly talented and knowledgeable people, and we just sit around and brainstorm until a viable solution is uncovered. I love going to the board to sketch ideas out, and I love sitting back and watching and listening to others as they jump up and do the same. The energy is high; creative juices are flowing; there are lots of jokes and laughter, and the overriding feeling in the room is "We can do this!"

If you have all these elements, and give the floor to the brainpower in the room, and give the group some loose facilitation to keep people focused—then that group will find your solution for you.

You must have, hold, and convey your absolute, unswerving faith and belief that there is a solution, and this group of talented people will find it.

I remember when I was in my first job as a programmer at Dynalectron. I was given a financial report, and told to 'fix it.' I went to the business user of the project to understand the problems with the report; she said it had calculation errors and gave me the corrections.

Simple enough, right? I made the corrections, but the report was still wrong. As it turned out, this report was an executive summary report, and it took data in from seven different input streams, e.g., Accounts Payable, Accounts Receivable, Sales, General Ledger, and so on. I found that literally each of these inputs had incorrect data, so of course, the executive summary report would always be wrong until I fixed these sources.

Technology was very different back then, and each fix was unique. One fix required that we go into the vault and pull out old backup tapes, and restore them. One fix required that we go into the microfiche library, find and print out five years of monthly reports, bring them to the business person who located and handwrote corrections on these, and then get them back and key in, line by line, every single number from those reports. One other input stream was missing intermittent monthly data that we couldn't recover from tape, so the fix was to arm myself with a calculator and sit down and manually figure out the missing data by subtracting older report numbers from newer report numbers ... and key in all those numbers.

It took months to find and resolve the entire thing, and apparently, it was worth it to Dynalectron for me to do it. The thing I remember most about this whole project though is when my boss came up to me one day when I was feeling frustrated at finding yet another problem. He said, "Barb, remember that computer is nothing but a stupid box. You can make it do anything."

That was a powerful concept to get so early in my career, and it has carried me far. Computers—all of Information Technology, to me—is nothing more than little bits and bytes, metal, and wire—and I can make it do anything.

So can you.

About six months before this, I had a similar experience:

In a company called Transettlements, I had an aspect of my job that involved calling repair people in if the computer went down. I guess my boss was thinking of this one day when he came up to me and told me his printer was down and I needed to get it fixed because he had an important report he needed to print within 30 minutes. I knew there was no way I could get a repairperson in that quickly, but he walked away before I could sputter out a response. I walked over to the printer, and stared at it thinking, *I don't know anything about printers. I'm not mechanical.* I turned the printer on, and watched it print a document.

Well, as I watched, I could see the paper was getting bunched up under the print wheel. I cleared it, set it up to print, and watched it bunch up again. I did this maybe five to six times, looking to see if I could spot what was wrong. And, guess what? I actually figured out the problem. I got a paper clip, unbent it, and then used it to tie two little flapping levers together, and voilà!, the wheel turned smoothly. I told my boss it was fixed; he printed his report on time; I called the repair guy in to make the permanent fix, and I walked back to my desk feeling so proud of myself I could burst. My lessons were: 1. Set high expectations—my boss just expected me to find a solution, and in the face of his faith in me, I met his expectations, rising above my own self-doubt. 2. I can solve anything—all problems have solutions.

These two little, but powerful professional experiences firmed up within me the belief that anything is possible.

I'm sharing these stories with you, because if you don't have the belief inside you that viable solutions can always be found ... then you need to develop such a belief. As a leader, it's not enough for you to fake it (though I recommend you fake it till you make it). You really have to integrate it, so you can exude it.

Then, pull the right people together—those with the knowledge of the problem and deep experience with the existing systems and operations. Give them the mission: Let's find the solution. Give them a loose facilitator—it can be you or someone else—to help them stay focused without constraining their brainstorming and creativity. Then, step back and let the talent fly, and trust that the group will find the answer.

While I'm often an active participant in these sessions because of my own skills and expertise, it's vital to give everybody else the floor. It's not my job to personally find the answer; it's only my job to make sure a solution is found. Especially on large projects, I clearly don't have the expertise needed to do it myself, so my job is to gather the right people, point them in the right direction, and then get out of their way.

One of my favorite movies is *Apollo 13*, directed by Ron Howard and starring Tom Hanks. It's the movie about the Apollo 13 disaster, in which pretty much everything that could go wrong, on a space flight, did. In one instance, the air filters weren't working on the flight, so the cabin was filling up with carbon dioxide and would soon poison the astronauts. There was another set of working air filters available, but they were round in shape and wouldn't fit into the square space where they were needed.

Believe Solutions Are Possible

Back in Houston, a project manager was given this problem: "You need to figure out how to fit a square peg into a round hole." He went back to his team of pretty geeky-looking technicians and said (I'm paraphrasing here): "We've been given this task, and we have to come through. We need to find a way to make this (he holds up the round filter) fit into this (he holds up a square item), using nothing but that (he points to a table full of miscellaneous items that the astronauts have available to them in their space capsule)."

Note the very clear direction, the faith in his team, and the commitment to find a solution. The next thing you see is the team immediately working together as an intent unit. You hear one of them saying, "The first thing we need to do is get all this organized," followed by another voice: "Somebody better put on another pot of coffee." The next thing you know, they have a solution.

I love this stuff! Project management is everywhere.

So, when you come across projects or programs that just seem impossible, my advice to you is: Assume they're possible. Get the right people. Share the problem with them, and the need, very clearly. Give them a place to play, and the tools they ask to play with. Keep them focused. Believe in them. Let them do their thing. Participate per your expertise, but don't overwhelm.

The solution *will* emerge.

CHAPTER SIXTEEN

TRACK AND RESOLVE RESOURCE CONSTRAINTS

Ugh! Resource constraints are one of the most constant issues I come across in projects, and one of the most time-consuming and relationship-dependent challenges we face as PMs. How do we make sure we get the right talent, and the right quantity of talent, to get the job done?

Chapter 2, *"Understand Your Incoming Team Members,"* covers key points you need to think through as you conduct your initial negotiations for resources. If you skipped that chapter, then go back and read it now—it's important.

In this chapter, I'll cover the various resource issues that come up as your project is underway. The question for this section is: How do we keep and fluidly adjust the type and quantity of talent needed to get the job done?

NOTE: I am not focusing on managing *non*-human resource constraints, e.g., budget, equipment, hardware, software, etcetera. You confront and deal with those constraints in your project planning and negotiations efforts: Either you either get the resources you need, or you negotiate a less-aggressive plan that will work with the lesser resources you'll receive. The actual procurement and installation of all these resources will be built into your project plan, and managed accordingly.

There are four common resource issues we will focus on here:
1. You lose a key resource because the person quits or, more likely, gets re-assigned.
2. You lose part of a key resource, meaning that person's time allocation to you gets reduced due to some other priority.
3. You need different resources, because the next phase of the project requires different skill sets.
4. You discover that a key resource is not viable in their project role, and you need to replace them.

There is another resource scenario you may face, but if you do, it's self-created: You have a transition in the project between phases that you have not adequately prepared for, so you have a week or two (... or three ...) lag time in which assigned resources aren't fully utilized, so they get attached to other initiatives and you lose them. If you're in this situation, then the solution will be the same as for (1) or (2) above. Aside from due-date pressure, this potential lag time threat to your human resources is another reason to always stay ahead of the game as the PM, and have just-in-time detailed plans in place so you're ready, and your leads are ready, for each phase transition.

LOSING A KEY RESOURCE

I fight like heck to keep all my key resources intact. The loss of project knowledge, camaraderie, teamwork, awareness of interdependencies, momentum, passion, and commitment of a key resource cannot be measured. Notice I didn't include 'skills' or 'talent' in this list: Equivalent skills and talent might even be available, but the loss of these other elements can create an immediate vacuum in your project that sucks life, energy, structure, and momentum right out.

Track and Resolve Resource Constraints

I engage in my battle to keep my key resource as soon as I get even a whiff that losing them is possible. I line up my bullets for why this person is invaluable to the project, and how losing them would cause X, Y, and Z problems. I lay out bullets showing how the loss of this person will cause missed due dates, and possibly move the whole project off track. I consider and bullet the reasons why replacing them with another person would not be sufficient. I review these bullets with my leads for their input, ideas, and suggestions.

Of course, I only go through all this if this information is factual and accurate: I go to bat for a resource when I absolutely know that losing them will hurt and endanger my project.

So far, I've used words like 'fight' and 'battle' to describe my approach to keeping my key resources. But, all this fighting is just a mindset that takes place off the negotiations table. I use this stance within myself and with my leads, as we think through the impact to the project if person 'X' is lost. I want to make sure I do all the work I need to walk into a resource negotiation, armed with exactly the information I need to win my case. My sole focus is: "We've all agreed the success of this project is important. Losing this person, at this time, puts the success of this project in serious jeopardy and I propose we retain them."

The person who wants to take my resource back is not fully aware, *until I tell them*, about how this loss will impact the project. Therefore, my negotiations need to be informational, not confrontational. That's why I take the time to pull together this information, in the form of simple, clear bullets. If I'm really concerned I may lose them, then I'll throw in a chart or graph to illustrate the impact, e.g., how a delay in a few related critical path tasks will extend the project deadline, or how the addition of a learning curve at this juncture will throw critical task 'ABC' off by three weeks.

I have one last vital step to do before I walk in to negotiate: I brainstorm bullets of several viable possibilities for the other person, showing how they can get *their* resource needs met, in some other way than taking back my person. If I get or keep this particular resource, it closes my (potential) resource gap, but it creates or extends a resource gap for the line manager. Sometimes the best solution for the line manager will be to backfill a lower position, and then have everyone below the project participant move up a level to take on the work of the person above them. Another solution could be to hire or contract someone from the outside, but it can be quite difficult to quickly find an external person with all the required skills, let alone institutional knowledge.

Remember: Put yourself in the other person's shoes. If some line manager believes they must have my matrixed person back, then I need to not only explain the consequential harm to my project, but I also need to help that line manager find a viable alternative to his or her resource problem. The case to present will be something like: "See how it's easier (or less risky) for you to get another resource for your needs than for my project to lose this one." If you truly need this particular person, then this case will almost always be true.

The actual negotiations are peaceful and objective: "Here are the facts that demonstrate why this person is vital to the success of this project, why losing them at this time would create too much risk to the success of the project, and here's how it will be better for the company to support you in getting your resource need met in some other way." This is win-win negotiations; it's respectful of the other person's needs, and it's responsible management of your project.

So, what happens if you lose the negotiations? You can always go above this person if you know the risk to your project is real and must be accepted by more people before the resource decision is final. I often do this. I let the first person know I'll be doing this. Sometimes I even invite them along, so together we can propose a better alternative for both needs to a higher decision-maker. If I've done a good job all along of laying out people's roles and responsibilities, especially who's accountable for what decisions, when I go above a person in a situation such as this, then I can just point to the project roles and responsibility charts and show how it's my obligation to let certain people know about decisions that put the project due date at serious risk. Remember, I'm an agent of the project, not the Sponsor, or key Stakeholders.

If all negotiations fail, and I end up losing that resource, then I negotiate as much cross-training time as I can, and with my leads, I quickly develop and implement a resource-transition plan. It doesn't have to be fancy, just clear and complete. My goal is to somehow still meet the project date, despite this setback. I add a bullet to all my status communications, written and oral, letting people know how this resource loss plays out. I want no surprises. It reminds people that we accepted new risks when we agreed to lose this resource, and now we're either able to overcome it, or we've had to change the scope or due date.

NEEDING NEW RESOURCES OR NEW SKILLS

This one is pretty clear-cut. Again, you'll need to plan and then do resource negotiations. The added challenge here is for you to do your resource planning far enough in advance, so you can lobby for resources, get them approved, get them off their current assignments and onto your project, communicate their roles and responsibilities, and then assign them to specific leads, who'll assign them their tasks ... all on track within your overall project schedule.

The more experience you have, the easier this is to do. You know every phase requires certain broad skill sets, e.g., analysis versus design versus development versus testing and training. So, at high level, you can be giving all your constituents a heads up that you'll be requesting and expecting these kinds of resources, at known points in time per the overall project schedule.

People will want to know time specifics immediately, so they can plan to meet your needs. This is completely reasonable, but often you will not know exactly what you need till the project is farther along. For example, you can likely say at the point you first create your high-level plans: "I'll need about a dozen people with 'XYZ' skills on a part-time basis starting in Phase III, and I'll need them at some level for the rest of the project," but you probably can't be as clear as "I need 14 people with 'XYZ' skills on a 30% basis for three weeks from xx/xx/xx through yy/yy/yy and then retain them on a 10% basis for the remainder of the project."

Build resource-planning tasks into your overall project plan, so you and your leads are triggered to stay ahead of your resource needs.

REPLACING A KEY RESOURCE

It seems I've had to replace at least one key resource on most large projects I've managed. It's always a challenge, because projects don't permit gradual resource decisions, nor do they permit time to grow an individual into a notably higher level of competency. You basically get the experience and skills people come in with, and these are either a fit for your needs or not.

If you are a project manager who actually has staff for which you have hire/fire authority, then of course you have time and responsibility *across projects* to help grow and develop your personnel.

However, in a matrix situation, which is the case on most large projects, your resources are initially assigned to you, often by others, and you get what they give you. While you usually have significant input into these decisions, you often won't know the actual people. You will be accepting the word of their managers that they have the skills you requested.

My advice to you is: Trust your gut. Look at the evidence. Move fast.

I touch on this topic strongly in Chapter 5, but I'll say it again here: One ineffectual key team member can cause enormous harm to your team, and to your project. Your best people will always step up to the plate to try to cover the slack ... but why would you make your best people do that?

The nicer and more personable the mis-skilled person is, the harder it is to let them go. Your other team members may even disagree with your decision. Nevertheless, you are accountable for the effective staffing of your team. You do this through your project negotiations initially, and you continue doing it in the ongoing monitoring and evaluation of people's performance and deliverables.

Track and Resolve Resource Constraints

Trust your gut. If you meet a person, and your initial impression is that they don't seem capable of doing what you need them to do, then trust that impression. Give them a couple of clear tasks that will let them quickly demonstrate their skills in action.

Look at the evidence. Look at the skills they demonstrate, and their results. If they deliver, great! If you have to replace them, then you will need to show their manager why they are not viable in their role. The best way to do this is to be able to point to a specific example, or two to three examples, of how the person did not deliver what was needed.

Move fast. Engage your Sponsor. One of the key responsibilities of your Sponsor is to make sure you have the resources your project needs. The Sponsor only knows about evolving resource needs if you communicate them timely and effectively. If you have a resource issue, you must get the Sponsor into the loop fast and provide them with compelling evidence and rationale so they can act if you need their help.

If you have a 90-day project, and it takes you three weeks to bring a person on board, clearly lay out their roles and responsibilities, assign them tasks, evaluate their effectiveness, and then make a decision to replace them ... you are already a quarter of the way through the project.

Remember, this is NOT the normal boss/employee relationship. This is a temporary, project matrix relationship. You are not firing the person because they lack skills, or can't be developed. You are replacing a person because they do not, right this minute, possess the quantity and quality of skills you need in the project role in which they are assigned.

Keep this replacement process objective. Know your bullets about why this person isn't working, and clarify your bullets describing the exact skills you need in the person you require as a replacement. Sometimes, you get assigned the wrong person because their manager did not fully understand what you needed. This is the time for you to make sure you're both clear on your needs. If you have a specific person that you want, then ask for that person by name, and explain why you want him or her.

Once the decision to replace the person is approved, and a new person is identified and approved, then you need a quick plan to effect the transition. With their manager, decide which of you should inform the person that they are being replaced. Usually, the person with the closest relationship can deliver the message best.

It's almost inevitable that when you replace a person, the replaced person feels upset. It *feels* like being fired—no question about it. It can be embarrassing to them, and they feel rejected. Nevertheless, if you know it's the right decision for your team and your project, then you must do it. The quicker you act, the better. Let the person know you made your decision based on your admittedly very quick assessment (you did), acknowledge the possibility that if you both had more time, things might be different (they might), and let them know your decision is final, and here's what you need from them as they transition off the project.

This is not easy. Not for you, not for the person who is being replaced, and sometimes not for your team if they really like that individual. But, when your decision is the right one, your team will experience the impact almost immediately. It is an enormous relief to have the right people in the right positions.

In my mind, it's good that decisions like these are hard. They make you think; they make you look for the truth, and they make you consider what's best for your team as a whole. I have zero regrets about any of these decisions I've made, though I can tell you each one was difficult. However, in each case, the benefit was immediate and long-lasting, and better served my team and my mission.

CHAPTER SEVENTEEN

MANAGE DUE-DATE PRESSURE

In Chapter 8, we covered setting and negotiating the project due date. In this chapter, we'll cover the daily pressures that exist as you and your team work to meet that negotiated due date. Even post-negotiation, your due date will still be and feel very aggressive, very tight, and very much at risk, since there will still be many known and unknown obstacles left to deal with.

USE YOUR PROJECT PLAN

Your project plan is the number-one weapon you have in your arsenal for relieving due-date pressure. You can do this in three ways, by using your plan as the basis for:

1. *Initial due-date negotiations with your Sponsor.* In typical negotiations, you will have presented three to four alternative high-level project plans and schedules, each with viable and unique mixes of scope, resources, and time. The outcome of these negotiations is that the business determines which mix of scope, resources, and time—meaning due date—it will fund.

2. *Communicating and managing the work activities of your team.* In status meetings, team members report their completion or progress against their assigned tasks in the plan. As team members meet their individual task due dates, you are meeting your project due dates.

3. *Engaging Sponsor and executive intervention as needed.* For example, "We've run into glitch 'X,' and it's pulling resources away from task 'Y.' As you can see, if this continues that task 'Y' will be three weeks late, which will make the whole project three weeks late. I need you to either resolve glitch 'X' or give me more resources in order for us to stay on schedule."

As the leader of your project, you must effectively pass due-date pressure on to your entire team. You all share responsibility for meeting due dates, individually and collectively. You need to make this clear. Communicate this concept with words, backed by action.

It's not enough to tell people their due dates. You must also share the reason for that due date, and why meeting that due date is vital to success. Often, you need to remind people why success is vital.

Do not underestimate the inertia of a company whose culture is to miss due dates, shrug shoulders, and point fingers at the other person. You, aggressively striving to meet your due dates, are *doing a new thing.* It requires your personal passion, drive, commitment, vision, and leadership to get people to move.

You feed people with this information: the reasons, the importance, the urgency behind what you are asking them to do. This is what speaks to people. People love a good cause; they love to be part of it, and they want to be on the winning team. It's up to you to show them your project has all these things going for them. Of course, you won't be convincing unless you are feeling these things yourself... which you can only do if you've stepped up to 100% accountability for the success of this project. Now, its success is your mission.

Your words are simple: "We will make this due date." You will be saying this over and over again to everybody you work with. You will assume it. It will come out of you in other words, too, such as "That won't work; we'd miss the due date. We need to find another solution," and "Great! If we do that, then we'll buy a few days we can use for task 'X' to make sure it gets done on time."

DEMONSTRATE YOUR COMMITMENT

More than your words, your team will be following your behavior. Since you have no tasks on the plan (at least on the large projects), you will demonstrate your commitment to meeting due dates by actions, such as:

- Meet your decision-making and communications commitments.
- Do what you say you'll do, when you say you'll do it.
- Be at meetings on time or early.
- Come to meetings prepared.
- Speak about status as it relates to the plan.

This last item is most important. Always talk and speak to your team members about their work as it relates to the project plan. When you get status updates, ask and speak about them as it relates to the plan: "So, how does this impact the plan?"; "Do we need to do anything to make sure we stay on track?"; "Do I need to get an executive decision for 'X' to make sure we meet this date?"; "Let me know as soon as it crosses your mind that we may miss an interim due date, so we can take action to make sure we don't miss it."

This seems obvious, I know. But, I've overlooked this myself from time to time, and every time I do, it takes away some of the urgency and momentum I've worked so hard to develop in my team. The responsibility for instilling a sense of urgency and momentum is mine. I share it with my leads, but they follow my example. If I slack off, then they slack off. If I get complacent, then they get complacent. If I treat the plan like it belongs in a drawer somewhere, then they do the same.

Own the Forest, Delegate the Trees

I don't particularly enjoy working with plans. It can be tedious to keep checking and re-checking with people to see how they're doing. And, I'm well aware nobody on my team really enjoys me checking at the task level to see whether they're on track or not. We're all responsible professionals, right?

But, I own the plan. And, since literally everybody else on my team DOES have tasks they need to execute, I am the only one able to keep my eye on the Big Picture: the plan. Every member of my team, since they have tasks assigned to them, is more likely to see their trees instead of our forest, because they have actual task work to do, and I don't. Enjoyment or not, they need me to do my job, which is to keep my eye on the whole plan and help them do the same.

In general, professionals (like most people) dislike someone looking over their shoulder and checking up on them. I don't blame them—I feel the same. So, I accept that I may get a resentful response from time to time, and I don't get bothered by it. I ask my team for status related to the plan anyway.

I try to honor them by keeping it matter-of-fact. ("Are any of these tasks delayed or at risk right now? No? So, all these tasks are complete, and these next ones are on track? Great!") Often, I'll read through each individual task item and confirm that it's on track. I am consistent; I ask these questions of ALL my leads, not just some of them. I ask them every week, at least. That's how I demonstrate my focus and commitment to the plan.

It's not enough to tell people to inform you if anything may go OFF plan. You must actively get them to confirm every item is ON plan. For some reason, it's my experience that the better and more dedicated your people, the less likely they are to give you advance notice that a task or set of tasks is in jeopardy. My guess is they're so committed, they keep trying in the face of all odds, and they refuse to believe they may miss a date until the date is actually upon them. By then it's too late, and you have lost the opportunity to take action to get that task ON track. People this dedicated aren't used to asking for help; you must create that opportunity for them by continuously confirming they are on track and obstacle-free.

I worked with a person years ago, who was the Project Manager of an IT team. He was one of the people I just described; so dedicated, he literally could not conceive of the possibility of failing to meet a project need. He was very challenging to manage, mainly because he always said "yes" to due dates, whether they were realistic or not. His team constantly failed to meet their due dates, and he was perplexed when I called him on it: He and his team were working all hours of the day and night; couldn't I see that effort? I ended up requesting and getting a new IT leader, because I needed to trust the status I was receiving. Most important, I needed to know when tasks were at risk, so I could step in and help find a solution.

I'd rather have a timely and accurate, "Hey, we're at risk for meeting this due date" for a status report than an overly optimistic, "Yes, sure we'll make it," any day of the week. The first gives me opportunity and options; the second ties my hands and creates crises.

By the way, the culture in many companies is for managers to deliver rosy status reports. So, when you are asking your team to let you know when tasks are at risk, you are often asking them to go against culture and tell you when things are NOT rosy. This takes repetition on your part, and understanding, and respect. People will start to fall in with this kind of routine project status communications, if you react to their status updates matter-of-factly, and work with them to resolve the obstacles they identify.

Do not blame. I've sometimes made this mistake, and trust me, it never works. First, I'm wrong to blame because effectively getting issues raised and resolved is *my* responsibility. Second, blaming accomplishes nothing, other than an erosion of trust. So, accept and then address issues that people raise to you, without blaming.

If you are a project manager reading this book, and you would like to explore these ideas, tips and techniques further, it may benefit you to let your manager and/or Sponsors know that Project Leadership Gold, Inc. offers training and coaching programs that are specifically designed to change on-the-job performance. When your company works with us, we will show how we measure, track and prove that the desired on-the-job behavior changes occur, and how those behavior changes result in quantifiably better project and business results. For more information, please point them to our website, and suggest they schedule a free 20-minute consultation to explore the possibilities: www.ProjectLeadershipGold.com

Section V: Your Toolkit

CHAPTER EIGHTEEN

TOOLS & LOGISTICS

The first thing I want to tell you here is that a key stumbling block for many project managers is that they often focus too much on tools and methodology. They look to tools and methods as absolutes: "If I follow this formula, then I will succeed. If I have the right tool, then I will succeed."

This is a very academic approach to Project Management. If you cling to it too tightly, then you'll be lost when your project hits a snag. It inevitably will. You'll find obstacles every day on your projects.

Tools are just tools. Methodologies are just tools. They are both just things that help you get the job done; they are not the job itself.

No project is a 'vanilla' project. Methodology and tools provide rough structure, some shareable communications mechanisms, and a degree of consistency between projects. But, the science and art of project management is about getting important business change implemented, through the focused talent of multiple people. Methodology and tools help you identify and address the more common elements and activities that exist between projects.

While you must master the common elements, it is even more important that you be able to rapidly and effectively address and resolve the *unique* elements. Each project is unique. The people and team dynamics differ in every project, even if just one person or one role changes. The problems, challenges, corporate constraints, priorities, business parameters, technical evolution, etcetera are different with every project. These are extremely fluid and dynamic elements. It is from these elements that crisis and unforeseen problems will pop up. Part of your skill set must be to proactively surface and resolve these 'non-vanilla' things.

People accomplish projects; tools and methodologies do not. Your ability to lead people is your most important skill set. This includes your ability to see and set a vision for your team, to inspire people to own that vision themselves, to clearly communicate the project goals and objectives and required results, to engage the right talent, to establish—with them—*this* project's path to success, to routinely raise and resolve issues, and to inspire, educate, manage, motivate, communicate, monitor, and track people's progress along the way.

That being said, let's focus on tools and methodologies here. I use the basics, and simple as they are, they've always sufficed for me. Here is a list of the tools I commonly use, with a few bullets or sentences about each:

(***Note***: *Samples of project tools, including many of the following, can be found at my website: www.ProjectLeadershipGold.com.*)

PROJECT BRIEFINGS

Your project briefings are a cornerstone for your communications throughout the life of your project. They are critically important, because projects move very rapidly and involve many people and many decisions. It's very hard for all parties to remember clearly how things evolved over time to bring the project to its current point.

Briefings contain the project's history, in picture-story format. They log the most vital information and decisions that impacted the course of the project along the way.

Your initial brief is where you list out the elements of the project charter: What's the business need? What's the purpose of this project; what was this project initiated to resolve? What, specifically, are the results the company expects to see and touch once the project is complete? Who are the initial resources, and what will they do first? Once you've run this by your Sponsor, and other Stakeholders, executives, and the Advisory Board if needed, this briefing contains the written, mutually agreed mission you and your team have been given.

Your second brief (the Negotiations / Solution Recommendation Brief) is the one that reiterates the project objectives, and describes your alternatives and recommended solution, with the background, pros, cons, and assumptions for each. It is the basis for your negotiations. Once you've presented it to all the key constituents, it will be updated to reflect the negotiated results including the mutual solution decision which your company authorized and you accepted.

The project kickoff brief usually contains a summary version of both previous briefs, plus it contains much more detailed information aimed at your project team members. This brief emphasizes Doer roles, responsibilities, reporting relationships, and 'here's how you'll each get started' information. Where your prior briefs were directed upward and outward from your team, this brief is specifically for your team members to introduce them to the project and give them a common vision, background, and context for their work.

Subsequent briefings will contain the progress updates, newly discovered issues, and the recommended and accepted resolutions to those issues, as well as the documented projected impact to the overall project plan, budget, resource allocation, and schedule.

Own the Forest, Delegate the Trees

PROJECT PLAN (HIGH LEVEL)

Strategically, your high-level executive plan is the one you will use throughout the life of your project, as the basis of your status reporting. To executives, this is the plan you are either on or off track with. Its size and level of detail, no matter the size of your project, is always one readable page. The high-level plan is your Level 1 plan. Here is a sample:

Level 1 Plan (Executive version)

ID	Task Name	Duration	Start	Finish
1	Financial Processes and Controls Plan	99 days	Mon 9/20/04	Thu 2/3/05
2	Launch project	3 days	Mon 9/20/04	Wed 9/22/04
3	Confirm or obtain required resources	2 days	Mon 9/20/04	Tue 9/21/04
4	Communicate plans to constituents	1 day	Wed 9/22/04	Wed 9/22/04
5	Identify Requirements	35 days	Thu 9/23/04	Wed 11/10/04
6	Identify Invoice and Reconciliation Requirements	20 days	Thu 9/23/04	Wed 10/20/04
24	Identify Financial Management requirements	15 days	Thu 10/21/04	Wed 11/10/04
33	Identify financial requirements in Governance	15 days	Thu 10/21/04	Wed 11/10/04
38	Design and Develop / Update Processes	53 days	Mon 10/18/04	Wed 12/29/04
39	Design & Develop Invoice & Reconciliation Process	30 days	Mon 10/18/04	Fri 11/26/04
56	Design & Develop Financial Management Processes	20 days	Thu 11/11/04	Wed 12/8/04
65	Design & Update Governance processes	35 days	Thu 11/11/04	Wed 12/29/04
70	Test Processes	37 days	Thu 11/11/04	Fri 12/31/04
71	Test Invoice and Reconciliation Processes	36 days	Thu 11/11/04	Thu 12/30/04
77	Test Financial Management Processes	17 days	Thu 12/9/04	Fri 12/31/04
83	Implement Processes	2 days	Thu 12/30/04	Fri 12/31/04
84	Rollout Invoice and Reconciliation processes	1 day	Fri 12/31/04	Fri 12/31/04
85	Rollout Financial Management processes	1 day	Fri 12/31/04	Fri 12/31/04
86	Rollout updates to governance processes	1 day	Thu 12/30/04	Thu 12/30/04
87	Provide Training	25 days	Fri 12/31/04	Thu 2/3/05
90	Perform Ongoing Management & Communications	99 days	Mon 9/20/04	Thu 2/3/05

Your Level 2 plan is your management bible, as the PM. Your Level 2 plan is one that shows the three to 10 sub-tasks for each Level 1 task. I can get most 90-day projects into a Level 2 plan of three or fewer pages.

Level 2 contains the detailed tasks you will monitor and track. This is the level you will ensure is maintained and updated within your team. This is the level at which you require status and issue updates *from* your team.

You report at Level 1; you manage at Level 2.

For most projects *over* 90 days, my Level 2 plans can grow to as many as 10 or a dozen pages. It's more unwieldy to maintain (so I usually delegate that to someone), but it's still pretty easy to manage because my leads are each accountable for specific sub-sections of the plan, and I can stay on top of things via my weekly one-on-ones with them. I do very elementary reporting only on the big plan, such as isolating any tasks that are late, or due this week or next week. These reports are just for me to help me stay focused as I meet with my leads and Sponsor.

PROJECT SCHEDULE

This is always a one-page graphic, and its purpose is to help everyone keep their eye on the due-date target. It shows just the major phases of the project, showing general phase sequences and overlaps. It also contains arrows pointing to the top one to five interim deliverables. These visual interim deliverables are key milestones for assessing the status of the project: If milestones are met / deliverables produced as per this schedule, then we are on track.

There are many ways to illustrate your project's schedule. Here is one I've used:

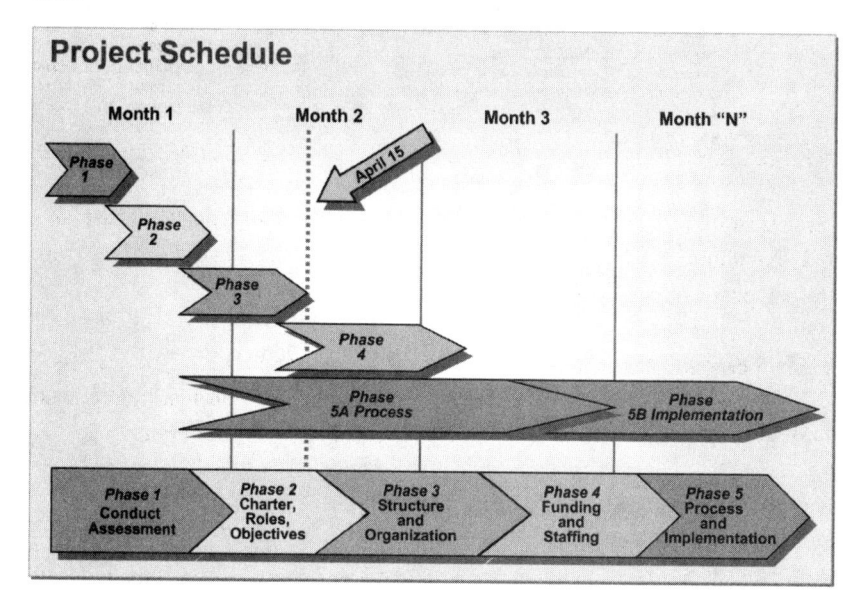

Project Schedule

	Month 1	Month 2	Month 3	Month "N"
Phase 1	►			
Phase 2	►			
Phase 3		►		
Phase 4		►		
Phase 5A Process	──────────────►			
Phase 5B Implementation				────►

April 15 (arrow pointing to Month 2)

| Phase 1 Conduct Assessment | Phase 2 Charter, Roles, Objectives | Phase 3 Structure and Organization | Phase 4 Funding and Staffing | Phase 5 Process and Implementation |

The project schedule above describes a project to design and implement a Program Management Office (PMO) within a company. The top arrows show the overall sequence of events; the bottom arrows describe the core deliverables of each phase, e.g., the deliverables of Phase 2 are the charter, roles, and objectives of the PMO. In this example, the "Month 'N'" section shows that implementation will take place over a number of months.

You can see how this graphic conveys the schedule from both a time and progress standpoint. This graphic is also a great picture to point to if you're trying to show someone the impact of some potential delay. Using the example above, if you foresee that obtaining the funding in Phase 4 might take two weeks longer than planned, you could insert a two-week potential-delay block that illustrates how everything else will also get pushed back two weeks. When you show people the Before and After schedule, it's a pretty powerful incentive for them to help you resolve the issue that could make that delay a fact.

PROJECT ORGANIZATION CHART

On large projects, I usually create two slides to show my overall project organization structure [*sample charts are shown in Chapter 3 "Project Organization Strategies"*].

The first chart I show highlights the Driver tier of my overall project or program organization. It focuses mostly on the relationship between the project team and all of its constituents, including the Sponsor, Executives, Governance, Advisory Boards, Stakeholders, Vendors, and Consultants. This is the organization chart that is my primary communications focus. These are the people I need to keep in the loop throughout the project. These are the people I will need to escalate core issues to, and negotiate with them for the best resolution.

I use the Driver tier chart to help me figure out the type and frequency of communications I need to establish between me and each of these parties. I also use this chart to remind me to support my Sponsor with strategic communication items, since the Sponsor is also accountable for various project communications to most of these same people.

The second organization chart I create focuses on the Doer tier: on the relationships in and among the team members. I use this chart primarily in planning, obtaining, maintaining, and transitioning project staffing. I also use it as a trigger for team communications, though on large projects it's primarily my leads who will be disseminating project information throughout the team.

The Driver tier chart rarely changes. The Doer tier chart often needs to be updated between the design and development phases.

Both charts are great as a focal point for any conversation regarding roles and responsibilities. The placement of boxes and arrows makes reporting relationships pretty clear. This lets the conversation focus on clarifying the details of what the role entails, what are the expectations, what will the actual work look like, what will deliverables look like, and how the quality of their work will be assessed.

PROJECT ROLES AND RESPONSIBILITIES

I prefer to show these as tiny bullets next to each box on the organization charts. However, there is often not enough room on organization charts to show the detail that's needed. If that's the case, I follow up my project organization structure chart(s) with a separate slide showing roles and responsibilities in table format. I use Word or Excel and list each role, with a bulleted list of its responsibilities next to it.

While most roles in a project are pretty generic, I usually do have to tweak this chart a bit with every new project. I only show roles that will be used by this project. I adjust roles as needed, usually based on the reality of the experience and skills of the people who are assigned to me.

For example, in large projects, I often need my Business Analysts to pick up some traditional project management functions—if the people have the talent. When I do this, I expand the BA role description for this project to reflect my expanded need and expectation. On some projects, I have to adjust the Sponsor role to reflect the reality of what my Sponsor will commit to doing. If the company gives the Sponsor title to someone who will not really be doing the role, I adjust the Sponsor-role description accordingly, and assign the true Sponsor responsibilities to whatever person will actually do them, e.g., an assigned BPM.

The documentation of these roles and responsibilities is important, for all the reasons listed in Chapter 2 *"Understand Your Incoming Team Members"* and Chapters 4 and 5 *"Work Effectively with Driver/Doer Roles."* Having these things in writing makes them real, and gives people a great, visual reference tool. It's still critically important that you or your team leads meet with all core team personnel, and personally ensure that they each understand and agree to their assigned role, and all the work it entails.

DETAILED PROJECT PLANS

As the PM of very large projects, you will usually not be working with really detailed project plans—your team leads will. It's your responsibility to know when more detailed plans are needed, to confirm your leads have developed them, and to ensure that they are using their detailed plans to manage the work.

In some cases, you may need to own some detailed plans yourself. This is a judgment call on your part, and you will make it based primarily on the degree of risk to the core project timeline. If I have no leads, obviously I own all detailed plans. While I have no rule of thumb for this, I have elected to own the detailed plans in projects where an extraordinary amount of detailed, dependent work needs to get done, by a large number of people from different organizations, in a relatively small window of opportunity. When failure in such a small window would cause the project to instantly and irreparably fail, it would be shirking my responsibilities to delegate this to someone else.

Tools & Logistics 203

The strategic value of detailed project plans is obvious: They give you visibility into the hands-on work of your project, which means you're very close to things and can almost instantly see when a threat arises. This means you can almost immediately resolve it, and keep things on track.

(*More information about project plans can be found in Chapter 7 "Time-Tested Structure and Routine."*)

ROLLING AGENDA

A rolling agenda is a fixed agenda that is used every time for routine meetings. The beauty is that while the agenda itself is fixed, it allows new, updated, and emerging information to roll through it each meeting. A good rolling agenda provides a connective tissue between meetings, so the action plans and decisions of one meeting are tracked and monitored in the next. These action items and decisions are documented in the Issue & Action Logs (*next tool*), which replaces more traditional Meeting Minutes.

Rolling Agenda

Meeting Agenda

- Confirm attendees
- State purpose of meeting
- Address agenda items:
  - Review agenda and add any critical topic items
  - Follow up any open issues from last meeting
  - Identify, document, and resolve or assign any open issues
  - Review all action items and assignments agreed to in this meeting
- Confirm next meeting date, time, location

- Shows people their presence or absence is noted
- Highlights chronic late or missing participants for resource tracking

- Helps people get focused

- Even though people see this same agenda every time, reviewing it helps people remember when their current 'hot topics' will be covered
- Writing peoples' current hot topics at the beginning of the meeting assures them these items will get addressed, and allows them to let them go and focus on the other agenda items as needed

- Provides continuity between meetings

- Ensures nothing falls between the cracks

- Gets a formal, public agreement of accountability

- Sets expectation of attendance
- Creates opportunity to resolve potential attendance issues

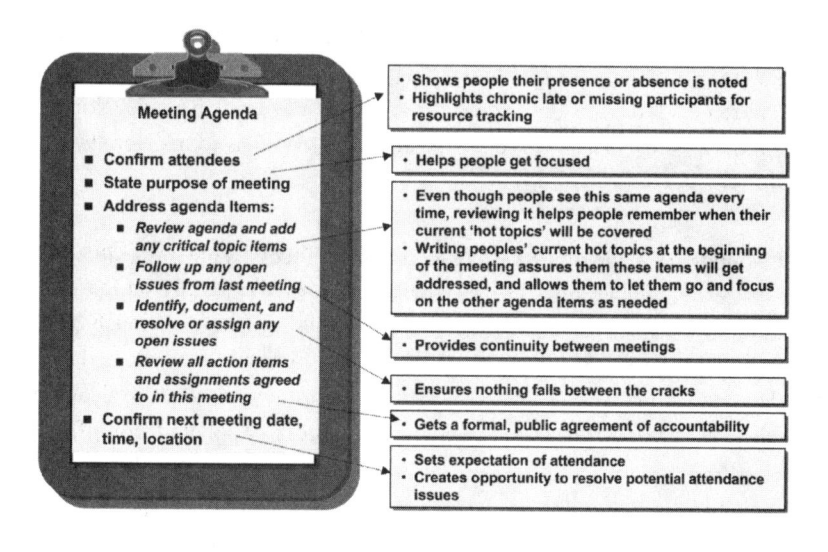

This sample rolling agenda above is focused on issue raising and resolution. I like my meetings to be about problem-solving and solution-creation: Meetings that only share status are historical in nature and don't move my project forward; meetings to just discuss things are purposeless and don't move my project forward.

If you want to combine status reporting with issue resolution, then you could add a 'Confirm each Team Lead is on track per task / per plan' agenda item after following up on open issues from the last meeting.

The strategic value of a rolling agenda is it gives you a simple meeting structure that you can implement with your leads, and they can implement with their teams. A rolling agenda is nothing new, but if you routinely use and adhere to one—that may feel new to many people. You will be setting a very high bar for your team in terms of what you expect from them in every meeting with you. When you facilitate your meetings in exactly the same way, when you ask the same strategic questions, it won't take long before people come to the meetings prepared to answer what they know you will ask. That is a pivotal moment on your team—it's the point where you know your leads now own their plans and responsibilities.

ISSUE & ACTION LOGS

Issue & Action Logs

Establishing and managing an Issue Resolution process is a core project management responsibility. The supporting tools to do this include the issue resolution process itself (steps, roles and responsibilities) and the Issue & Action capture and tracking log.

*The **Issue Resolution Process** and the **Issue & Action Log** are covered in Chapter 10.*

MEETING CALENDAR

I put together a meeting calendar for large projects so that everyone can see and plan around each other's routine meetings. It helps everyone remember their own standing meetings. It makes it easier to schedule ad-hoc meetings around these.

Meeting calendars also let everyone involved in the project see when key leaders are getting together to review progress, discuss issues, or report status upwards. If team members have issues that require escalation for decisions or problem-solving, they can raise these items to appropriate meeting attendees in advance, and know these items will get addressed in the next meeting. Routine meetings are the best way to make sure issues are surfaced and resolved proactively.

Month XYZ

Monday	Tuesday	Wednesday	Thursday	Friday
1 8-9AM Communications Team Meeting 8-9AM Tech team mtg 1-2PM Sponsor & Barb	**2** 9-10AM Team Lead Status & Issue Resolution Mtg	**3** 7-8AM Sponsor & Barb breakfast	**4** 8-9AM Tech team mtg Noon – Status & resource updates to Barb 1-4PM One-on-One status update 45-min	**5** 10:30-noon Sponsor Mtg wt Team Leads 2:00PM Weekly Status distributed
8 8-9AM Tech team mtg 1-2PM Sponsor & Barb	**9** 9-10AM Team Lead Status & Issue Resolution Mtg	**10** 7-8AM Sponsor & Barb breakfast	**11** 8-9AM Tech team mtg Noon – Status & resource updates to Barb 1-4PM One-on-One status update 45-min	**12** 10:30-noon Sponsor & Barb 2:00PM Weekly Status distributed
15 8-9AM Communications Team Meeting 8-9AM Tech team mtg 1-2PM Sponsor & Barb	**16** 9-10AM Team Lead Status & Issue Resolution Mtg	**17** 7-8AM Sponsor & Barb breakfast	**18** 8-9AM Tech team mtg Noon – Status & resource updates to Barb 1-4PM One-on-One status update 45 mins	**19** 10:30-noon Sponsor Mtg wt Team Leads 2:00PM Weekly Status distributed
22 8-9AM Tech team mtg 1-2PM Sponsor & Barb	**23** 9-10AM Team Lead Status & Issue Resolution Mtg 2-3PM Monthly Status briefing to Advisors & Stakeholders	**24** 7-8AM Sponsor & Barb breakfast	**25** 8-9AM Tech team mtg Noon – Status & resource updates to Barb 1-4PM One-on-One status update	**26** 10:30-noon Sponsor & Barb 2:00PM Weekly Status distributed

On the calendar, I include the standing daily, weekly, & monthly meetings that my key leads and I are required to attend. I usually just set up and print a special Microsoft Outlook calendar for this, or I create one using Word or Excel. I list the time, day of week, and the name and/or purpose of the meeting. Sometimes, I list required attendees. I make sure this meeting calendar prints legibly on a single page.

PROBLEM-SOLVING PROCESS

I've been very lucky throughout my career in being able to work alongside some excellent consultants.

Each consulting firm walks in the door with their own private label methodology for addressing and resolving business problems, via projects. I have seen, discussed, debated, questioned, used, and evaluated each of these methodologies. After all the bells and whistles, they break down to a simple, consistent, core problem-solving process. It's common sense-structured.

Remember, as the PM, your role is to drive others to do the right work. This problem-solving process is the framework and basic sequence of activity through which you drive your team:

1. Understand the Current Situation
2. Define the Desired State
3. Identify the Gaps Between the Current and Desired States
4. Identify Alternative Solutions that Might Close the Gaps
5. Select an Alternative
6. Implement the Alternative
7. Evaluate the Results

I have been consistently effective using this basic approach in all my projects, large and small. We tend to think big, complex problems require big, complex ways of dealing with them. But, what we really need is a simple, logical, structured way of thinking our way through the problem to get to the best solution.

This problem-solving process is that simple way; it is important for you to know and internalize it. I carry this seven-step checklist in my head and use it as a touchstone to help me understand where I am and where I need to lead my team regarding a particular problem. If you would like a more detailed walkthrough of this process, you can find a quick and re-usable Problem-Solving tool for this in my website: *www.ProjectLeadershipGold.com*.

FACILITATION TECHNIQUES

There are common 'types' of brainstorming and planning you will do with your team in each project. These include problem brainstorming, solution brainstorming, prioritization, general task identification and sequencing, and process evaluation. I recommend you learn at least a handful of specific facilitation techniques to help you guide a roomful of people to consensus.

Facilitation techniques enable you to guide your team through structured, focused thinking. They help prevent unnecessary and off-point discussions, while they free people to be creative, inventive, and expressive.

In addition to learning how to run some structured sessions, you'll also want to learn basic meeting facilitation skills. These include things such as how to keep groups focused, how to get yourself out of the way, how to quietly direct attention away from one person and towards another, and so on.

I regularly use facilitation techniques I learned years ago as part of some Total Quality Management (TQM) training I received. You can find many books and courses on TQM facilitation techniques on the Internet. General meeting facilitation tips are available in the "Meetings" section of the PM Gold! Tip Booklet, see Chapter 18 *"Tools & Logistics."*

MASTER CONTACT LIST

A Master Contact List is a simple spreadsheet listing the names, titles, companies, project roles, and viable contact information of everyone on your team, from the senior-most executive to the last hands-on team member. If your team is spread out geographically, you may want to add a 'time zone' column. I usually delegate this list to someone else to create and maintain.

The most important thing is that the contact information be current and accurate. Make sure people give you numbers where they can actually be reached: Having a corporate desk number for a traveling consultant will obviously not work; you need their cell, pager, or Skytel number. If you know you need to reach people after hours, make sure you capture their 24-hour and weekend contact information. Use weekend contact information wisely, but have it readily available in case you need it.

This Master Contact List gets distributed to your entire team. It's a pivotal tool for your people to quickly identify both who they need to contact for something, and how to reach them.

If you have special contact needs, e.g., an over-the-weekend implementation, then make sure people update this list with their contact information for that particular weekend, e.g., a key 'on call' expert may be visiting relatives in another state that weekend, and you'll want a new land line in addition to their cell phone, in case you have cell-reception problems. Redistribute this list to your team as often as makes sense, depending on the frequency of updates.

A note of caution: Since this Master Contact List DOES get distributed to so many people, you do need to be careful about the personal contact information you are publishing. Some people, for valid reasons, will not want you to ever publish anything other than their company phone and company e-mail data… even though you really need their cell phone data and home phone numbers in some projects. You must honor their privacy, and NOT publish that secondary data.

The best way to make sure you do not step on anyone's privacy is to start your list with only 'official,' readily available business contact information. Then, send out an e-mail requesting whatever additional contact information you need, and let people know to whom you plan to distribute it. Most people will give you the extra contact information. Those that prefer not to do so will let you know.

MEETING MINUTES

I rarely use meeting minutes because in my experience, meeting minutes are rarely read by anyone. They typically do not contain clear or actionable information, so they are not useful in driving the project forward. Instead, I use the Issue & Action Log (*see Chapter 10*). It is an easier and more functional 'what we covered' document than traditional meeting minutes, which are basically a transcript of what everyone in the meeting said.

Some companies require meeting minutes though. Here are some guidelines to make them more effective for you:

Meeting minutes should be as short and succinct as possible. Generally, they contain:

- Meeting name,
- One-sentence meeting objective statement,
- List of meeting attendees, with the Facilitator or Leader flagged,
- Bullets of any key decisions made,
- Bullets of any agreed-upon action items, including the task, to whom it's assigned, who else will participate, and when the action is due, and
- Note any scheduled follow-up meeting(s), dates, and times.

In my experience, meeting minutes don't follow the above format. Instead, they contain a rambling narrative of what was said in the meeting. The shorter and more action-oriented you make them, the more useful and readable they will be. Think "bullets, not paragraphs" and "one-page max."

STATUS REPORTS

The status report is a formal, written, highly visible, one- or two-page document through which you:

- Convey the current status of your project relative to your timeline,
- Convey your resource usage to date (people, budget) relative to the resources you were allocated,
- Provide your best estimate of whether your project will remain within your timeline and resource allocations, or whether it will exceed them by 'X' amount, and
- Raise critical issues to attract senior attention and drive specific remedial action.

On large projects, there are often a couple of very big issues brewing for which you need an executive decision to clear your path. People will respond to published, visible warnings even if they haven't responded to previous warnings you have tried to share via voicemails, e-mails, and personal drop-ins.

Don't raise flags on things you already have under control. If you do so, you will only create the "Boy Who Cries Wolf"[26] effect.

Let's talk about your Sponsor and status reports. Your Sponsor is above you, and if your project has big issues, your Sponsor will be held accountable for those as well as you. Before you publish an issue, you had best be sure that a) you've given your Sponsor solution recommendations and the opportunity to fix the issue first, and b) you have been clear and up front with your Sponsor about all the ramifications if that issue stays open, including the fact that you'll have to report it.

---

[26] By "Boy Who Cries Wolf" effect, I mean that every time you grab executive attention for unnecessary items, you lessen your chance of grabbing their attention when you really need it. Let executives know that you value their time; only engage them after exploring all other reasonable avenues first.

Issue resolution is your job. One of your most important responsibilities to your Sponsor is to keep them in the loop, so they can help you keep the project on track. Ideally, when an issue hits your published status report, it's because you and your Sponsor *together* are raising it to senior executive attention as part of your joint strategy to get the issue resolved.

But, absolutely, no matter what your Sponsor says, report the facts of your project's status as you see them. This is your report. It is your personal statement to the company as to whether or not your project is on or off track.

In most companies, raising flags within a status report is a cause for alarm and possible strife. People dislike hearing bad news. People dislike giving bad news. There may be some degree of pressure to give a rosy status report, when you know the project is really in danger. Again, you must report the facts as you see them. Stick to the facts; that is your duty.

I don't like writing status reports. I find them painful and time-consuming. However, I have to admit the very act of putting the status of my project in writing makes me see very clearly where I may or may not be doing everything I need to do to close my issues. I don't want to report an issue that I should have been able to get resolved.

Usually, I draft my status report at least one day before it's due. Often, while writing that draft, I realize I have to either close a specific issue or report it. Since I'd much rather close it than report it, I go close that issue if at all possible.

In this way, writing my status reports is the self kick-in-the-pants I need to resolve something I have allowed to remain open. This same kick-in-the-pants factor also works when I share my draft status report with my Sponsor (I recommend always providing draft status reports to your Sponsor). Often they, too, will step up and complete something they need to do, so that we can avoid publishing it as an open issue.

In large projects, one of the best outcomes of written status reports is that they force a routine meeting-of-minds between you and your Sponsor. Ideally, the two of you are in sync all the time, but in some projects, this cohesion just doesn't happen. When the two of you sit down to discuss what to tell others about your project, it forces you to discuss the question: Are we on track, or is this project in danger? If you have sub-projects, I recommend you discuss each of those, and assess a status for each as follows:

- <u>"Red" status</u>: This item is currently off track, and we will miss the end date unless we immediately take corrective action 'X.'
- <u>"Yellow" status</u>: This item is currently off track, and there is some risk of meeting the end date. It is either too early to decide to take corrective action, or we've already taken corrective measures, but it is too early to know if they will be successful.
- <u>"Green" status</u>: This item is currently on track, and looks good for meeting the end date.

After you've assessed each sub-project, you can now more accurately make a status assessment of the project as a whole. In general, if any of my sub-projects are in "red" status, I put my whole project into "red" status until that potential showstopper has been resolved.

I remember having this status discussion with one of my Sponsors:

The facts of our situation were that while everyone was focused on implementing mandated *technical* system changes, many, many *business* process issues kept surfacing on the side. These business issues were requiring a great deal of human resources to address. I recall my Sponsor looking at me and saying, "I feel like we're facing a dike, and we've got our fingers and toes busy plugging up holes, but the damn thing's still leaking. I'm questioning how it is that everything's apparently so broken in my department."

We had a great discussion about this, because he was right—it absolutely felt that way. We were forced to look back and figure out how we got to this point. What we saw was that the scope of business process change required in our project was far larger than anyone in the corporation had realized. As we talked, we saw that our project was effectively re-engineering my Sponsor's entire business process, via radical changes to underlying customer interactions and technical systems.

Once we saw this, we realized we needed a more comprehensive approach to the business process changes than we had in place. We put that plan together, then we were able to share the whole thing—problem and solution—with others, so they could see it, too. The end result was that our due-date never changed, but the scope increased, and our project processes and resources were uplifted accordingly. All key people involved supported and approved these changes.

Without the requirement of formal status reporting, I don't know how long it would have taken for my Sponsor and me to see what we needed to do differently. Even for leaders, it's challenging to step back and remember to look again at the Big Picture. Factual status reports, and the formal and routine nature of them, are extremely powerful tools for the PM, because they force you to do this higher-level thinking and situation-assessment on a periodic basis.

WAR ROOM

I have two words for you on this topic: Get One. For large projects, your team absolutely needs a good-sized meeting room they can call home. If your team is geographically spread, then consider war rooms for each key location. Team members need an always-available place where they can hold ad-hoc meetings, and where they can write things on boards and flipcharts and then go away for a few hours and come back to pick things up again.

You need a war room for the duration of the project. You'll be personally in the room a lot in the front-half of your project, when you're in the project planning and solution design phases. Your implementation team(s) will be using the room more in the second half of your project, as they do their technical design and planning work.

I know meeting space is limited in most companies, and that getting a war room for the duration can be a challenge. Nevertheless, your team is matrixed and often virtual; it needs at least one physical 'home base' that everyone knows about and can rely on. Reliable physical togetherness is pivotal to teamwork, rapid communications, and momentum. Create it whenever it's practical.

Projects demand ad-hoc meetings, because project plans are created based on estimates and assumptions that only time and further analysis will validate. As new information surfaces on a daily basis, people will need to share this new information, and find ways to address it that keep the project on track. To have two-hour, four-hour, 24-hour delays, or more in holding these meetings simply because no meeting space can be found is unacceptable. Such delays will add up quickly and throw your project hopelessly off track. Don't let something this simple create frustration and risk for your team. Get them a room.

Large projects often require other dedicated space in addition to a War Room. Some examples include:

- For some initiatives such as ERP (Enterprise Resource Planning) implementations or Agile[27] projects, you might want separate work space—whether cubicles or individual offices that are co-located—for the PM, the project administrative support person, project leads, and other key project participants. This allows them a work area, separate from their regular office, where they can focus on the project without interruption from co-workers from the department or group where they are based.

- When introducing a major product, process, and/or system change, you may want to secure dedicated training space for your project. This is valuable when you have a lot of people to train, and you need to train them in iterative cycles.

---

[27] Agile methods, very loosely defined, provide a conceptual framework for approaching software engineering projects that generally involves working projects in shorter, iterative work segments, involving and engaging many skill sets along the way, co-locating resources as possible, and emphasizing software performance as the primary measure of progress.

- For outsourcing or merger and acquisition initiatives, you may need to set aside a set of dedicated meeting rooms for representatives of each company during the time period in which legal negotiations are taking place. Each party will require privacy, and a secure space in which to keep confidential documents.

EMAIL

E-mail is a curse and a blessing, as we all know. I had one bright, shining period of time where I had two administrative assistants at once, and one of them would read and filter all my e-mail for me, so I only had to deal with a relative handful a day.

Those were the days!

Spam aside, project managers still get an extraordinary number of e-mails every day. You need to establish your own systems for dealing with it all, or it will steal ridiculous amounts of your time.

My personal incoming e-mail strategy is this:

- The last thing I do at the end of each business day is to handwrite a simple "To Do" list for my next day of the things I must get done.
- I get to my office 30-60 minutes early, look at this list, and tackle whatever highest-priority items I can before my day really gets started. I do these first, so I make strategic progress before addressing whatever urgent or potential-crisis items may be sitting in my inbox.
- Then I check my e-mail. I quickly delete what I can. I forward e-mails I can delegate, with a brief message letting people know why I am forwarding this e-mail and what I want them to do when they read it. I answer some e-mails immediately, in quick but clear bullets. I move the rest to a 'holding' email folder for me to review and tackle at the end of the day.
- At the end of the day, I repeat this process, except I also clean out my 'holding' folder.

Throughout the day, I send out a lot of e-mails. When I do, I'll also skim my inbox for e-mails I'm expecting, and for those coming from my Sponsor, key leads, or other strategic people who may need quick answers or decisions from me to keep critical things moving.

When you write e-mails, remember each and every one of them is an opportunity for you to move your project forward. Be clear, and provide the small, important details. Don't just forward things and expect people to know what you want them to do—add a sentence that tells them. If you're asking them to get in touch with you, then give them a due date and time, and some clue about the topic.

One last point: Don't engage in e-mail battles with people. Putting arguments in writing is risky; e-mails often come across much more harsh and stubborn than you mean. Worse, they encourage the other person to e-mail their argument back, and that's just another e-mail for you to deal with. If someone sends you a complaint, argument, or debate-type e-mail, in most cases, then it's best to just send back a simple e-mail or voicemail saying, "Thanks for your feedback. I'm going with (direction ABC) because (single-bullet explanation). If you have any further questions, please contact me in person and we'll talk." Use your own words and personal style, but keep it very short, acknowledge you've received what they sent, and give them the option to contact you again in person, and delegate responsibility for any such further action to them.

Even if it may seem like an e-mail response would be quicker, in argument or complaint situations it's usually much quicker to deal with it face-to-face. Since you've delegated the next step to them, they'll only create a follow-up with you if it's truly important to them. If they do, then don't allow it to be scheduled for more than five to 15 minutes. In this amount of time, the other person can see you are listening; you get the chance to see how serious the issue may be, and if further action is needed, you will know it. You can also make sure you both leave the meeting on good terms, which is important relationship management.

If the complaint or argument comes from your Sponsor, or from someone who may bring the complaint to your Sponsor directly if you don't deal with them effectively, then you need to respond more fully. Your team needs you to keep problems out of their way, and communications is your primary tool for doing this.

VOICEMAIL

Pretty much everything I just wrote about e-mails applies to voicemail as well. I prefer e-mails to voicemails, so I let everyone know this, which eliminates a lot of incoming voicemail for me.

If any of my project team members tend to leave long, rambling voicemails, then I'll ask them to plan their messages in advance, so that they leave short and clean messages. In general, if team members or loosely-affiliated people leave vague voicemail messages like "Call me," then I'll either not respond (if I don't respond, and it's important, I know they'll find another way to reach me), or I'll respond and let them know I won't respond to messages like this going forward. I do this because a 'call me' message doesn't give me enough information to assess urgency. Again, there are exceptions to every rule, and if executives or key influencers leave vague messages ... I will respond. It's a matter of trying to positively control that which I can.

ADMINISTRATIVE ASSISTANCE AND DELEGATION

While administrative assistants seem to be much less available than they used to be, having one is critical for your large projects. When you combine reaching and coordinating people through e-mail, voicemail, pagers, BlackBerry devices, and tools like MS automated scheduling systems with trying to grab rooms in which people can meet, that all adds up to lots of administrative overhead by your key players, including you.

You need to have an administrative person who has your whole project as their Number-One Priority. They will:

- Schedule meetings and rooms, including all contacts, attendance confirmations, cancellations, and re-scheduling.
- Manage all logistical items, e.g., conference calling, whiteboards, flipcharts, audio-visual equipment, office supplies for the team, travel arrangements, etc.
- Maintain and/or distribute your standing documents, e.g., Master Contact List, Project Meeting Calendar, Issue Logs, Project Plan, and so on.
- Provide the above services for your key leads as well; this is very important.
- Be your point of contact when you're in meetings and unreachable; they can manage and limit daily interruptions for you.
- Screen calls, e-mails, and mail for you.
- Remind you of upcoming management activities and deliverables, e.g., routine status reports.

In large projects, it's easier and more cost-effective for the company to funnel all these things through a single person, rather than spreading them out to everyone on the team. Projects move too fast, and have too many people trying to do too many different things. If there's no one in the middle helping coordinate all this, then meetings will be scheduled on top of each other all the time; this will create tremendous lag time within your project schedule. Even when using tools such as Microsoft Outlook's calendar and schedule features, which do help a lot, a large amount of cancellations and re-scheduling still occurs.

The amount of administrative work in large projects is huge, and you do NOT want your principals buried in it: It's a surefire recipe for failure. Put an administrative resource on your project organization chart when you need one; determine what percentage of time you need from them, and then request and negotiate for that resource as you do for all the others.

POWERPOINT

I know studies have shown again and again that PowerPoint presentations are pretty boring and not that memorable. Nonetheless, PowerPoint is still the tool most companies use for their briefings, so it's worth your time to become very comfortable and handy with it.

The key to a successful PowerPoint briefing is to a) tailor it to your audience, and b) make sure your briefing has a purpose and that it achieves that purpose.

Tailor Your Briefings to Your Audience
- If the reviewer is a graphics person, then use graphics in your briefing. If the person likes words, then use words. If you don't know their preferences, then ask them or ask the people that regularly report to them.
- If it's an executive briefing, then keep it short and very high level.
- If it's a status briefing, then make sure it tells a story.
- If it's an informational briefing, then make sure you've anticipated the questions people want answered, and then build those answers into the briefing.

Have and Achieve a Purpose with Each Briefing
- In all briefings, you want an action from the audience. That action is usually one of three things:
    1. A specific decision from the reviewer(s),
    2. Approval of the briefing contents and recommendations, or
    3. Confirmation that the information in the briefing is sufficient for the audience to work with.
- Make sure you know what action you want from your audience, state it up front in your briefing, and ask for it specifically at the end. Then, wait till you get it, or work with your audience until they are able to deliver the action you need.

There are amazing add-ons for PowerPoint now that allow you to include audio, video, and animation effects to your briefings. In general, avoid adding bells and whistles to your briefings—you don't have that kind of time. But, in some situations, these features are not bells and whistles—they're vital to your effective communications program.

For example, most PowerPoint briefings themselves are not at all self-explanatory. To make sense, they need you to add verbal details and transitions while you walk people through each page. But, if you have a very large audience, spread across different locations, working in different time zones or work shifts, then it's difficult or impossible for one person to personally deliver project information to everyone. If you can record the delivery of the briefing, and make that A/V recording available, then the extra time it takes to create that briefing will pay for itself in the saving of your personal time to deliver.

PM GOLD! TIP BOOKLET

This is a fabulous little booklet you can use for instant and actionable refreshers and extensions of key project management information in this book. Tactical tips are included for these topic areas:

- Putting a Team Together
- Typical Roles and Responsibilities
- Project Plan
- Project Negotiations
- Performance Measures
- Meetings
- Manage Time

At my website, *www.ProjectLeadershipGold.com,* you can find the PM Gold! Tip Booklet. Keep it handy, so you can find quick ideas when you need them most.

SOME CLOSING THOUGHTS ON TOOLS

In my first few projects, I did actually try to maintain a lot of the above-listed documents in a project binder. It was helpful in the beginning while I was internalizing the basics. Now, I just organize all these elements within various folders in my computer.

In addition to all the tools listed above, here are some other tools you may need to consider on a per-project basis:

- As the PM of large projects, you don't need these, but your teams may: flowcharting tools, software development tools and methodologies, design tools, and estimation tools.

- As the PM of large projects, you may need these, or your company may require your team to use or abide by these: portfolio management processes and tools; policy and procedure documentation methodologies; internal and external audit requirements; various state, local, federal, industry regulations; approved IT architecture standards. (If you don't know what any of these last items are, or when and how to use them, then ask other PMs in your company to see which of these items are relevant for you, and where to find your company's selection of them.)

I also suggest you look to PMI (Project Management Institute) or Rita Mulcahy for general project management assistance.

Section VI: Your 9-Step PM Checklist

Overview

This whole Section VI is your project management Checklist. It contains a high-level summary of your key management responsibilities within a project, and specific tips and notes for each.

The intent is that you can come here at any point in your project and be able to find something immediately useful to help ground you and guide your next steps.

Where applicable, you will see cross references to the related background and explanatory information that is covered in more detail in the previous five sections. You can quickly refresh yourself with those as you choose.

INTRODUCING THE NINE STEPS

You have already seen the following chart that shows your overall responsibilities as a project manager. As a refresher, in Section II, we covered the left-most column "Create, Engage and Manage Your Team." In Section IV, the focus was on the right-hand "Resolve Ongoing Challenges" column.

In this section, Section VI, we'll cover the items in the middle "Manage Project Lifecycle" column. You can see that the activities in the "Manage Project Lifecycle" column are fairly sequential. This means you can plan your work for these activities according to the same sequence.

I have broken this work out into nine different steps, based on my own experience with how the work tends to cluster itself. The focus is on the core steps and activities of the project *manager*... not the steps and activities of the project team as a whole.

226 Own the Forest, Delegate the Trees

Project Management	
Manage Project Lifecycle	**Resolve Ongoing Challenges**
1. Clarify deliverables and targeted results 2. Plan analytical phase 3. Obtain and launch analytical resources 4. Drive viable solution alternatives 5. Prepare and negotiate alternative implementation plans 6. Obtain and launch implementation resources 7. Manage business process and technical systems design 8. Manage development and testing activities 9. Manage implementation and evaluation	**Constant Crisis** • Issue Resolution Process **Environmental Barriers** • Corporate politics, culture, and priorities • Resistance to change **Relationship Glitches** • People and personalities • Communication pitfalls **Persistent Problems** • Solution complexity • Resource constraints • Due date pressure

Create, Engage and Manage Your Team

In the segments which follow, you will read about each of the nine core steps PMs must execute per project. For *each* step, you will be given:

- Step Description
- Key PM Deliverables and Objectives Checklist
- Your Activities
- World-class Strategies for Success

STEP 1: Clarify Deliverables and Targeted Results

Description:
This is where you, personally, make sure you understand everything you need to know about this project. You do this through meetings, thinking, reviewing all relevant documents, thinking, having initial discussions with your assigned leads, and did I mention thinking?

Key PM Deliverables and Objectives Checklist

- ❑ Understand exactly what is expected of you, your team, and the project.
- ❑ Clarify and document scope, goals, objectives, resource parameters, and any known or suspected obstacles.[28]
- ❑ Clarify and verify the communication needs & expectations of the key people within your Driver tier.
- ❑ Get a clear, tactical picture of the political and cultural lay-of-the-land in which your project will play out.
- ❑ Demonstrate your leadership capabilities to the project's executives, specifically that you know what you're doing, you're in charge, you understand their needs, wants, and demands and you're prepared to find a way to deliver them.
- ❑ Establish an excellent relationship foundation with the highest, pivotal people that must be pleased with your results.

Your Activities

- **Perform relationship-building** and information-gathering via a series of meetings, primarily with the key executive Stakeholders, your Sponsor, and other strategic influencers you identify (e.g., consultants, customers, representatives, vendors).

---

[28] This collection of information is often referred to as the "project charter." Project charters come in many flavors, but the common factor is that the project charter captures a clear, written description of what you and your team are to accomplish, and the parameters and constraints within which you'll be working.

- **Conduct information-gathering via reading**. In many cases, you'll have access to a Project Charter or a Decision Package—a collection of the written material that has been put together to justify this project.
- **Do information gathering via thinking**. Think about the questions you need answered, identify who knows the answers, and then go get the answers. Think about the people involved, what you know about them, how they relate to each other, and how these existing relationships could help or hurt your project. Think about strategic things you know about the company, e.g., what are the big initiatives out there that you foresee will be taking executive attention away from your project?
- **Do information gathering via your gut**. This is the time to pay close attention to what your gut is telling you. If it's sending up serious warning signals, then ask the questions to find out if these warnings are valid or not. Don't assume you know the whole game until your gut agrees that you know the whole game.
- **Identify your leads**, assigned or not.
- **Identify your desired "right-hand" person** as soon as possible. This is the person who needs to know most of what you know, so they are able to fill in for you in certain situations as needed. They can also be your key lead working downwards within your team. [*While I invite my right-hand person to some of my key meetings throughout the project, I do not bring this person with me to my initial executive meetings where I want a one-on-one relationship focus.*]
- **Share what you know** about the project, players, resources, risks, constraints, and challenges with your identified leads. Together, determine what high-level information you still need before you can complete your plans to flesh out a solution. Assign that information gathering among yourselves and then begin that research.

- **Brainstorm "next steps"** with yourself and/or your leads. Working from the assigned due date backwards, break the work you imagine into high-level phases.[29] Estimate the duration of each phase, and figure out how much time you have before your need to be sitting in front of your Sponsor with some viable plans and solutions. Identify any additional information you need to know before you can get to that point.

For More Information
- Review the Advisor and Sponsor-related segments of this book (*Chapter 2 "Understand Your Incoming Team Members" and Chapter 4 "Work Effectively with 'Driver' Roles"*).

World-Class Strategies
- ✓ Be able to demonstrate you know what you're doing and you are capable and in charge. At the same time, know and demonstrate that you are an agent of the project, and a subordinate to your Sponsor and key executive Stakeholders.
- ✓ Stay at the executive level throughout this phase. You need to be thinking and speaking about the things executives care about. You need to speak in the language they speak. Do not fall into solution-finding or techno-speak in this step. You are not a technician speaking; you are a leader and project management expert, talking to fellow leaders. You are not finding the solution; you are gathering the information you need as PM to develop a plan for a team to go find the solution.
- ✓ Achieve and communicate an optimistic can-do attitude, while also acknowledging unknowns, obstacles, and risks exist.
- ✓ Get yourself into top-notch, high-speed mental, emotional, and energetic gear instantly. You must immediately lift yourself up to your own peak, because it's your job to inspire and uplift everybody else.

---

[29] For more information on managing this due-date dilemma, read Chapter 8 "Master Your Due-Dates," Chapter 9 "Get in the Game of Negotiations," and the Project Sponsor section within Chapter 4 "Work Effectively with 'Driver' Roles."

STEP 2: Plan Analytical Phase

Description
Your team's first major deliverable is to find a viable solution, with alternatives. You will be presenting these in a briefing in Step 5. This step, 2, is where you *develop your plan for finding that solution*, and get approval of that plan from your Sponsor, and other key Stakeholders as needed.

Key PM Deliverables and Objectives Checklist

- ❏ Develop your high-level (one- to two-page) project plan and schedule.[30]
- ❏ Determine your approach and the resources you will need to find a solution.
- ❏ Fully engage your key leads.
- ❏ Ensure the relevant executive tier has a mutual understanding of your project's purpose, objectives, immediate resource needs, and the date at which you'll come back to them with a viable solution and final plan.

Your Activities

- **Identify your desired core leaders**, ask for them, and get them now. Very often, these leads will be allocated to you already, so this task may be moot. In some situations, though, you may know your allocated leads aren't qualified or sufficient, so you need to immediately negotiate for the ones you want. Negotiation techniques might include asking for proven leads elsewhere in the company, or asking for external consultants.

---

[30] If you have a short project and a small team, say less than three months' duration and three-ish people, then your plan and schedule can and should be detailed and crisp in this phase. If you have a larger project and/or more than three people, then you still need a solid overall *schedule*, but you may only have detail *plans* for early phases. This section assumes you are not using an 'agile' approach, which maps out work in 'sprints' versus 'phases,' with each sprint being fairly isolated and complete in itself. Even when using an agile approach, as the PM you still need an overall project plan and schedule, within which you'd create and manage detailed work lists ("backlogs") per sprint.

- With your leads, **develop your approach to finding a solution**. You'll need to think about the *work* of the project to see what business and technical functions and systems may be impacted by your project. You'll need to clarify your assumptions about what the core elements of your solution might be, and at a very high level also clarify the biggest obstacles, risks, and unknowns.

- With your leads, **identify the specific people who need to be involved** in finding a viable solution. These will be the key experts on the existing processes, and the key drivers of the upcoming change. Consider if you also need meeting facilitators, or administrative and documentation support.

- With your leads, **develop your plan, schedule, and project organization chart**. Create a detailed analytical phase staffing chart, showing needed individual FTEs and activity duration. Identify other resource needs for this analytical phase, e.g., analytic software tools, war room, etcetera.

- **Craft your first briefing** for your Sponsor. The first few slides will repeat your understanding of the background and purpose of this project. The remainder of the briefing will be to lay out your plans for the analytical phase, giving a due date for when you will be able to present a viable solution and solution implementation plan. Your objective is to obtain approval of your plan, approach, and resource request.

- Tweak and **present this briefing** to other key Stakeholders. Your objective is to a) Make sure that you and your key Stakeholders have a clear, mutual understanding of this project and your objective, b) Get these people to approve your resource requests and release their people to you as you've proposed, and c) Build credibility and trust by showing a quick and well-thought out plan for how and when you'll nail down a solution.

For More Information

- Skim Chapter 17 "*Manage Due-Date Pressure*," Chapter 9 "*Get in the Game of Negotiations*," and the first six tools in Chapter 18 "*Tools & Logistics*." This will give you a Big Picture refresher and help you get clear on what your team's analytical work needs to deliver.

- Skim Chapters 4 and 5 "*Work Effectively with 'Driver/Doer' Roles*" and Chapter 6 "*High-Voltage Resource Planning*" as guidance to help you clarify your project's resources needs.

World-Class Strategies

✓ Make the personal decision that "the buck stops here." This is the step in which you shift from accepting *assignment* of the project to accepting and *owning accountability* for the project.

✓ Achieve both excellence and speed. This is not a period of eight-hour workdays. In my projects, this is where I kick my butt into very high gear and work to get the exact people I need, and develop a plan and approach that will uncover a solution as fast as humanly possible, that I know I will deliver.

✓ Maintain the appropriate relationship with your Sponsor and executives. Your Sponsor and the executives most likely see a hierarchical superior-to-subordinate relationship. You need to keep meeting them where they are, while owning that you are the project management expert and the daily leader of this initiative. This is especially challenging at the start when you are establishing your core relationships.

STEP 3: Obtain and Launch Analytical Resources

Description

In Step 2, you obtained approval of your analytical phase plan, schedule, and resources. In Step 3, you need to go get those resources, introduce them to the project, and get each one of them started on the right foot.

Key PM Deliverables and Objectives Checklist

- ❑ Get the right people assigned to participate in the analysis; obtain their managers' agreement and commitment to the amount of participant work time you are requesting.
- ❑ Establish urgency and momentum in your core leads, Stakeholders, and newly assigned analytical team members.
- ❑ Demonstrate you and your key leads have a very firm and calm handle on the project already.
- ❑ Communicate, clarify, and lock in core roles, responsibilities, and relationships of your key team leads and business/technical experts. (*Though your main focus is on the immediate analytical work, for those people who will be with you and the project long-term, provide your expectations of them for the whole project.*)

Your Activities

- **Gain the agreement and commitment** of each Stakeholder and each individual assigned resource. On large projects, your key leads may obtain some of these agreements and commitments for you.
- **Inform participants of their project assignments**. Per assignee, first identify the best person to tell them of their new role. Usually the best person is their boss who will tell the person they've been assigned to your project, tell them what their time commitment is, and direct them to speak to you for specific information about what they'll be doing for you. Some Stakeholders will naturally offer to do this, but often you'll need to tell them: "I need you to let your people know about their assignments by close of business today. I'll send them a Welcome e-mail this evening and let them know the next steps."

- **Schedule and conduct meetings with new assignees.** The first objective is to welcome them and help them feel comfortable with their role and assignments. The second objective is to make sure they understand their role and assignments well enough to execute them with excellence.
    - For key people, such as high-level business and process experts with specialized knowledge and input, I prefer one-on-one meetings, and I prefer doing them myself versus delegating them. It's an early opportunity for me to learn more about these people, and it's a chance for them to share their needs and concerns with me.
- **You *may* create and present a project kickoff briefing**, especially if your project is large, your team is large, and/or your team is geographically dispersed. Kickoff briefings are a good way to get everyone on the same page quickly, to let everybody see everybody else, to get a feel for the size and importance of the project, and to be struck by the fact that, yes, this project is officially launched.
- **Work very closely with your leads throughout this phase.** You all need a shared brain in this phase, and consistent messaging. It's very important that you be a cohesive leadership team already, in front of everyone else, even if behind the scenes you are all still scrambling a bit to get ahead and stay ahead of the game.

For More Information

- Skim Chapters 4 and 5 *"Work Effectively with 'Driver/Doer' Roles"* and have your key leads skim them, so you can all be clear and consistent when communicating role and responsibility information to your team.

World-Class Strategies

- ✓ Be organized in advance.
- ✓ Have your key leads already in sync with you, in advance.
- ✓ Get your Sponsor and Stakeholder to support you, and work on the project's behalf themselves, by releasing needed resources from their current workload immediately, so they are available to work on your project now.

STEP 4: Drive Viable Solution Alternatives

Description

This is where the team does the business and systems research and analysis, and develops a recommended solution plus alternative solutions. The previous steps have all been to *get your leads and your team ready* to do this work. Analysis is done through meetings, thinking, a review of all relevant documents, thinking, initial discussions with your assigned or possible leads, and—you guessed it!—thinking.

Key PM Deliverables and Objectives Checklist

- ❏ Personally demonstrate and expect commitment to the solution goals and belief that this group will find great solutions. Focus on facts and experience versus emotions, structured thinking and analysis, and big, creative thinking.
- ❏ Facilitate and drive your team to identify three to four viable solutions that will meet the goals of your project, on schedule and on budget.
    - ○ Capture the issues and assumptions that lie behind each alternative.
    - ○ Capture the pros and cons of each alternative.
    - ○ If you are unable to find three to four viable solutions within your given time, budget and resource constraints, then document in clear, bulleted points which issues or assumptions are the key stumbling blocks you and your team could not resolve. (You must still provide three to four 'best' alternative options.)
- ❏ Analyze your alternatives, identify which you will recommend as 'best' and document the pros and cons of your recommendation.

Your Activities

- **Manage your core leads**. Your core leads are the people who will be accountable for driving the analytical work to be accomplished, including the between-meeting research and data-gathering work.

- **Facilitate key work sessions**. Facilitation is an excellent way to drive people through the structured thinking processes that are most efficient in getting to great solutions.
- In work sessions, and with your leads outside work sessions, **design "straw model" documents** to help people 'see' the deliverables they are shooting for.
- Communicate, communicate, **communicate with your Sponsor** throughout this whole period. The more informed your Sponsor is throughout this step, the easier the negotiations step will be, and the easier it will be for the two of you to tell the company why the resulting solution recommendation is best.
- **Your team will:** Understand and document the "as is" business and technical processes that relate to your project. Understand and document the "to be" business and technical processes. Identify the gaps, prioritize them, and brainstorm solutions to close gaps. Prioritize those solutions and do a 'deep dive' into the most promising.
- **You and your leads will** be involved in all strategic sessions; review all key in-progress deliverables, facts, and findings; keep things on track; manage people and their activities to the plan.
- In the background, you will **be building your Negotiations briefing**, section by section.
- **Schedule the briefing review and approval meetings** between you and your Sponsor, and between you, the Sponsor, and the Advisors.

For More Information

- Read Chapter 8 *"Master Your Due Dates"* and Chapter 15 *"Believe Solutions Are Possible"* to help you set the right stage for this work.
- Skim Chapter 9 *"Get in the Game of Negotiations,"* so you can start mentally preparing for how you will make a solution recommendation, and explain and justify your supporting analysis.

World-Class Strategies

✓ Stay ahead of the team, vision-wise and task-wise.

✓ Pay very close attention to all people and relationship issues that pop up.
  - They are often subtle in this stage; many of your people don't know you and are more comfortable sharing their issues with others. You need to be constantly opening the door to people, inviting them to share a concern, and showing them respect and objectivity when they do.
  - Approach techniques: "Does anybody see any problems or obstacles to what we just discussed?"; "Is there anything we've forgotten?"; "Is there any reason I shouldn't go out and start telling people what we just decided?"; "I'm meeting with our Sponsor today—is there anything I should know before I do?" and so on.

✓ Discover the right working relationship between yourself and each of your leads. Prior to this, you've all been planning and thinking together. This is really the first time you are leading others through *their* leadership. It's important that you establish the MO (Methods of Operation) for your team, while respecting the working style and preferences of your leads. I often do special one-on-ones with my leads in this period for us to nail down the specific behaviors of how we'll work together.

✓ Create the recommendation materials so cleanly and brilliantly, and line up the executive approval sessions far enough in advance, so you have greased the path to achieve fast approvals in the next step (Step 5) and thus maintain your project's momentum.

STEP 5: Prepare and Negotiate Alternative Implementation Plans

Description

In this step, you will document, present, and obtain approval of the recommended solution and plan you developed in Step 4. Concurrently, you will prepare to launch the next three project execution steps, and begin working to obtain the funding and resources needed to complete your project.

Key PM Deliverables and Objectives Checklist

- ❏ Obtain mutual agreement between you and your Sponsor(s) on the final combination of scope, resources, schedule, and budget that you commit to deliver.
- ❏ Support your Sponsor in obtaining mutual agreement between the Sponsor and executive Advisors on the final combination of scope, resources, schedule, and budget that you commit to deliver.
- ❏ Actively engage your key leads in preparing for the implementation stage that is just around the corner. While you're completing the negotiations briefing, they are figuring out how to transition between the analytical team(s) and the implementation team(s) and exactly how to bring new people on board.
- ❏ Begin working within your company's processes to obtain the capital and expense funding required and approved.
- ❏ Complete your *detailed* project plan, resource plan, schedule, and budget.
- ❏ Establish your weekly monitoring and measuring procedures for tracking actual progress against approved scope, schedule, budget, and resource allocations.

Your Activities

- **Complete the Negotiations briefing** which you began building in Step 4.
- **Conduct negotiations** and update the negotiations briefing with the project scope, resource allocation, and time schedule to which you and the executives mutually agreed.
- Guide your team leads to **plan and prepare to launch the implementation stage**. This includes planning the communication of roles and responsibilities, welcoming new people on board and introducing them to the project and the progress-to-date, showing everyone the overall implementation plan and schedule, and meeting with individuals to clarify their personal tasks and due dates.
- **Build an implementation Kickoff briefing**. You'll be able to pull most of it from your Negotiations briefing and your first briefing from Step 2. You'll need to add information about the back-end of the project, and address the questions and needs of the implementation resources.

For More Information

- Read Chapter 9 *"Get in the Game of Negotiations"* for an in-depth look at the creation of a negotiations briefing and the strategies of negotiations.
- Read Chapter 13 *"Pay Attention to People and Personalities"* for ideas on how to best present your recommendation to appeal most effectively to your approvers and decision-makers.

World-Class Strategies

✓ Be a proactive partner with your Sponsor. The company will look to the Sponsor to give them the solution they want; the Sponsor looks to you to have the detailed rationale and answers regarding the solution you are presenting. Make sure the Sponsor is engaged and informed sufficiently, so the Sponsor also owns and stands behind your joint recommendation.

- ✓ Drive the approval process. Executive decision-makers are overbooked and peripherally engaged. You must obtain their time and show them clear and complete data, so they will give you fast and excellent decisions.
    - Create a great briefing. This item is pivotal. The briefing covers so much material it could get very long very fast, but you need to keep it as short and succinct and as factually, logically persuasive as possible.
    - Know your audience: their fears, hesitations, vision, desires, roles and responsibilities, and political situation. You are not negotiating with one blob of people, even if you're sharing the briefing with a group. Be fully prepared to clearly touch on the talking points that each audience member must hear in order to be comfortable and confident in saying "Yes" to your recommended solution. Put yourself in their shoes and ask, *"What's in this for me? What does this mean to me?"*
    - Stay open to new information that could change or revise your recommendation and related plans and activities. While it's rare, sometimes there is hot-off-the-press information that necessitates changes.
- ✓ Get your leads to start up detailed implementation planning while the recommended solution is pending approval. You must maintain momentum and excitement within your team in this decision period.

STEP 6: Obtain and Launch Implementation Resources

Description

Once you've gotten your implementation phase plan, schedule, and resources approved, you need to go get those resources, introduce them to the project, and get each one of them started on the right foot. This is almost exactly the same work as Step 3, but often you have far more people assigned to implementation work than to analysis work. These people may be several levels deep within the company, which requires going through more layers of managers to reach them.

Key PM Deliverables and Objectives Checklist

- ❑ Get the right people assigned to participate in design, development, and implementation; obtain their managers' agreement and commitment to the amount of participant work time you are requesting.
- ❑ Clarify roles and responsibilities and confirm mutual understanding and expectations.
- ❑ Establish urgency and momentum in your core leads, Stakeholders, and newly assigned implementation team members.
- ❑ Demonstrate that you and your key leads have a very firm and calm handle on the project already.
- ❑ Personally demonstrate and expect: commitment to the implementation, belief that this group will meet the due date, ownership of tasks and results, and early notice and resolution of issues.
- ❑ Initiate an issue resolution process.

Your Activities

- **Share the implementation plan** with key constituents.
- **Clarify and/or re-clarify roles and responsibilities between yourself and your key leads** for the work remaining on the project. On large projects, the team leads usually act as project managers of their own piece(s) of the plan. Your job is to make sure they are consistent with each other, that they each have a detailed work plan which you've discussed and approved, and that they report to you against their plans. You will minimally have a weekly meeting with your leadership team, which may be the issue resolution meeting, or may be a separate check-in, planning, and decision-making meeting.
- **Implement and communicate the issue resolution process**.
- **Begin leading routine status and issue-escalation meetings** with your Sponsor.
- **Initiate ad-hoc communications.** For example, create small briefings for your Sponsor for critical updates, prepare talking points to explain certain core issues to Sponsor, Stakeholders, or Advisors, and so on.
- **Identify and plan for ongoing project communications**, e.g., status reporting and interim briefings or updates.

For More Information

- Read Chapter 5 *"Work Effectively with 'Doer' Roles,"* and have your key leads read it, so you can all be clear and consistent when communicating role and responsibility information.
- Read Chapter 10 *"Activate the Issue Resolution Process"* for how to establish and manage an issue resolution process.
- Read Chapter 16 *"Track and Resolve Resource Constraints"* for tips on how to recognize and resolve potential resource issues.

World-Class Strategies

✓ See the Activities from Step 3; they apply here.

✓ Re-confirm existing resource commitments. Do not assume that people remember and still plan to honor resource assignments they made when the project first started. Go back to the managers and Stakeholders of your current resources, thank them for the resources they've made available so far, and let them know how much time you still need from those resources, for how long.

✓ Many people still equate the word 'project' with 'technical project,' as long as any IT people are involved. Business people who think this way often fail to recognize the business process implications which they will need to address. These include changes to jobs, reporting relationships, skill sets needed, tools and reports, customer interactions, inter- and intra-departmental relationships and interactions, etcetera. You will likely need to help the managers of these business functions step up, plan for, and manage these changes.

  o Many business people aren't familiar with project management methods and tools, so they don't have effective ways to lead and implement change on this scale.

  o You want these managers to drive these changes under your project's umbrella, so you can coordinate activities and resources.

  o In general, business people respond very well when you provide structure and process for them. You just need to make sure you and your leads make the time to do extra communications and even some training around this.

STEP 7: Manage Business Process and Technical System Design

Description

Back in Step 4, you and your team created a high-level solution design, which was developed *just far enough* to prove to yourselves that it is viable. This step, 7, is the detailed design step. It's where you and your team will discuss, decide, and document exactly what the 'end game' business and technical processes will look like.

Key PM Deliverables and Objectives Checklist

- ❏ Drive the efficient development of the business requirements, per the project plan.
    - ○ Ensure the documented requirements will, once implemented, deliver the targeted business objectives.
    - ○ Get signoff on the business requirements from key Drivers (to include the Sponsor, key Stakeholders, Business Analysts, key SMEs, and technical leads). Sponsor, Stakeholder, Business Analyst, and SME signoff indicates, "Yes, if these requirements are implemented, then the business targets for this project will be met." Technical lead signoff indicates, "Yes, these requirements are clear and appear complete; they are sufficient for my team and I to use in building an excellent technical design."
- ❏ Drive the efficient development of the business process changes and technical systems needed to meet business requirements, per the project plan.
    - ○ Ensure the business process and technical systems solution design will deliver the targeted business objectives.
    - ○ Get signoff from the Business Analyst, key SMEs, and key Stakeholders on the proposed business process changes and technical solution design. Signoff indicates, "Yes, this business process and/or technical system design appears to meet the requirements I approved."

❑ Manage your team leads to rigorously follow the plan and schedule, and proactively seek, raise, and resolve and/or escalate issues as part of the issue resolution process.

❑ On a weekly basis, monitor, capture, and report on your project's status, specifically show 'approved versus actual' schedule, resources, and budget. Explain any deviations from plan, and the actions you are taking or requesting to get back on track, and the impacts if you are unable to get back on track.

Your Activities

- **Inspire, direct, push, and pull people to execute the plan**; your team is doing the work.
- **Clear the path for your team** to achieve their due dates.
- **Maintain team focus on design work**. This is a design phase. Do not start developing the solutions until all parties know exactly how the end solution will look, feel, and function. If you skimp on this step (and you will get pressure from many sides to do so), then you may as well start adding big bucks to your budget and plan on moving back your due date. Skimping on this step never saves time; in fact, it adds money and adds time. Make sure your team:
    - *Drives the design to a low enough level of detail* that shows specifically how the end solution will look, feel, and function. This clarifies and validates the high-level solution design.
    - *Documents the design clearly*, so other people can pick it up, understand it, and 'make it so.' Design documentation serves as the checklist of what must be implemented. It also serves as an audit trail for understanding the whole solution as well as its individual pieces.
- **At strategic points, bring your Sponsor and key Stakeholders into business process design review sessions**. Have their project SMEs in the room, and facilitate a walkthrough of the design, showing how things are now and how things will be changing as a result of the project. The hat everyone wears in these sessions is 'business process flow,' not technical system flow.

- **Manage and enforce basic project management structure and disciplines**: manage key leads and team members to plans; manage the issue resolution process; perform or oversee routine and ad-hoc project communications up and down the line.

For More Information

- Skim Chapter 7 *"Time-Tested Structure and Routine"* and Chapter 12 *"Manage Resistance"* for information you can use to help you establish and maintain basic project management structure and disciplines within your team.
- Read Chapter 14 *"Be a Compelling Communicator"* for ideas about how to manage the day-to-day people issues and situations that come up in projects.

World-Class Strategies

✓ Manage scope. Many new big issues and opportunities surface in this step. You and your team will need to drive to the decisions that allow you to meet the due date with high quality. Clarify 'must-have' versus 'like-to-have' scope elements.

✓ Keep design work at the right level.

✓ Keep your technical people fully in the loop and engaged, while ensuring business personnel and business needs drive all core solution design elements. Don't put the technical constraint brakes on too early in the design phase.

✓ Meet due dates. You are the #1 Driver to the due date. You must be relentlessly committed, and you cannot talk about dates enough. People won't like this; they'll grumble and get irritated ... but you have to do it anyway. If 10 people out of 50 turn in one task two days late, your project has lost 20 days of work, or one FTE (Full-Time Equivalent) month. On large projects, tiny misses spell disaster very rapidly.

- ✓ Get people to surface threats and risks to you before they grow into issues and problems. Your team is heads-down; you need to keep asking the questions that will help them remember to tell you about fermenting items.
- ✓ Handle issues calmly, with elegance and grace. You do this by staying focused on the facts. The facts are just the facts; they're neither 'good' nor 'bad.' Keep yourself and your team focused on the facts, and you'll see the best possible solution for every problem, and the best way to explain both the problem and the solution to others.
- ✓ Probe for issues frequently and consistently. Putting out fires is a core function in this step, so the excellence of your issue resolution is key.

STEP 8: Manage Development and Testing Activities

Description

This is often the longest single step in your project. The solution was designed and documented at the detailed level in the previous step. In this step, 8, your team will create the tactical, physical system and processes that will be implemented. Services get documented. Formal customer communication materials get created. Job descriptions get written and all aspects of organization re-structuring are decided and prepared. Programs are coded. Software, hardware, and equipment are acquired and installed. Products are developed. Training occurs as needed. All project deliverables are completed. Completed systems, tools, and processes are tested.

Key PM Deliverables and Objectives Checklist

- ❏ Continue to monitor, capture, and report on your project's status each week. Show 'approved versus actual' schedule, resources, and budget. Explain any deviations from plan, and the actions you are taking or requesting to get back on track, and the impacts if you are unable to correct.
- ❏ Manage your team leads and members to the project plan.
- ❏ Drive and manage the proactive raising and resolving of issues as part of the issue resolution process.
- ❏ Meet the project due date.
- ❏ Ensure all deliverables meet or exceed business requirements.
- ❏ Personally sign off that all deliverables, collectively, will deliver to the business exactly what it wants and expects, per negotiations.
- ❏ Ensure that test participants understand and sign off that test results demonstrate that developed business processes and technical systems meet requirements.
- ❏ Develop the detailed project implementation and rollout plans.

Your Activities

- **Inspire, direct, push, and pull people to execute the plan.**
- **Clear the path for your team** to achieve their due dates.
- **Manage and enforce basic project management structure and disciplines**: manage key leads and team members to plans; manage the issue resolution process; perform or oversee routine and ad-hoc project communications up and down the line.
- **Manage the Big Picture.** Keep looking ahead to make sure every detail is in place for the actual rollout.
- **Maintain, obtain, and protect your resources.** (I almost put this as a World-class Strategy, but this is a time-consuming activity on most large projects, so I list it here for you to expect and plan for.)
- **Communicate consistently and well.** Ensure all impacted parties—internal and external—appropriately understand and are ready for the coming change(s).
- **Manage the development of implementation and rollout plans**, including exit strategies in case initial implementation tasks are unsuccessful.

For More Information

- See Section IV for a list of the common project issues and obstacles and how to resolve them.

World-Class Strategies

✓ Stay in the forest, not in the trees. In this phase, literally, your whole team is heads-down working their tasks and their part of the plan. You are about the *only* person who is tasked with holding the Big Picture. You need to keep talking about 'what happens next,' and 'after we complete these steps we'll be into this next section of the plan.'

- ✓ Get thorough, detailed test plans that all players buy in to.
- ✓ Maintain project structure and discipline. Technical people tend to be much more familiar with project structure and process. Most of them have worked with software development methodologies, design and estimation tools, and so on. Nevertheless, they are as likely as anyone else to resist working within your plans and structures, so stay on top of task status.
- ✓ Probe for issues frequently and consistently. Putting out fires is a core function in this step, so the excellence of your issue resolution is key.

STEP 9: Manage Implementation and Evaluation

Description

Implementation is when the switch is turned 'on' and all changes take affect. Implementation can occur all at once, or it can be phased.

Key PM Deliverables and Objectives Checklist

- ❏ Manage the rollout of project deliverables into the business and information technology production / live environments.
- ❏ Achieve an error-free implementation, so when the switch turns 'on,' everything and everybody are working perfectly.
- ❏ Meet or exceed business requirements.
- ❏ Complete useful, documented identification and communication of Lessons Learned.

Your Activities

- **Ensure all players know their exact roles**, and the timing and dependencies of all tasks.
- **Conduct implementation plan walkthroughs** with all participants.
- **Develop plans, including resources, for post-implementation support.** For example, make sure there are people available for some specific period of time to address problems that occur due to the implementation.
- **Prepare and execute a handoff from the project team to the support team** who will own it going forward.
- With the Sponsor, **obtain all 'Go' approvals from identified decision-makers.**
- **Manage the execution of rollout plans.**
- **Monitor post-implementation support activities.**

- **Conduct a project evaluation**. I do a very simple evaluation:[31] I have the key project players come together for a couple of hours, and we a) Brainstorm and create a "What Went Well/What Didn't Go Well" list, b) Prioritize the "What Didn't Go Well" items, and then c) Brainstorm solutions to the top three to five issues. That information gets documented and communicated, with those solution recommendations.
- **Close down the project**. Celebrate your team as publicly as you can. Provide performance reviews and letters of commendation. Ensure incentives are delivered. Collect all key project materials and documents, create backups as needed, and store as required.

World-Class Strategies

✓ Coordinate all rollout details.

✓ Ensure all needed communications occur.

✓ Keep resources for post-implementation support and project evaluation, when other projects will immediately want and need them.

✓ As an ideal: With the Sponsor, close the business loop by measuring the *business* results of the project. I've never seen this measurement activity on any project plan, largely because business results often don't begin to be realized until after the project is implemented. Measuring the *business* results of projects is generally accepted as the business's responsibility, not the project team's ... but it rarely takes place, and is even more rarely published. However, an on-time, on-budget project is only a true success when it delivers the original targeted business results, e.g., increased revenues, decreased run-costs, increased market share, and so on.

---

[31] I know there is a constant and growing push to do more thorough evaluations. I support that, but have found in practice that many companies simply don't allocate the time and resources to do this. The simple approach described here surfaces excellent information, fast.

CHECKLIST CONCLUSION

That concludes this Checklist section. I hope you noticed that each segment takes only a few minutes to skim. You have the option to spend more time if you choose to follow the 'For More Information' cross-references.

I recommend you come back to this section of the book from time to time throughout your projects, even if you are an extremely experienced project manager. If you do this, it will give you the benefit of at least one other person's thinking, as you do your planning and strategizing activities.

You'll benefit in at least one of these two ways:

1. You will either feel very comfortable that you already have the key things covered, or
2. You will notice something you overlooked, and you will add it to your list.

Section VII: Incredibly Motivating Conclusion

FINAL WORDS

For the 'incredibly motivating' part, please play the theme from *Rocky* as you read the following:

Every book has to end somewhere, and this one ends here. Part of me wants to keep going because there is *so much more* to project management than I've been able to cover here. But, a bigger part of me is thrilled to have completed this book, so it can be shared.

I hope you have been able to find something in here that is useful to you. Maybe it's a new concept or idea or tool. Maybe it's a new tip or technique for more effectively engaging with the people you work with every day. Maybe you didn't find anything new here, but as you read through this, you could recognize and validate some of your own experiences and reflections.

In any case, I hope you felt my appreciation and respect for you as a fellow project manager. I know your time is precious and limited; thank you for spending it with me and this book. I am truly honored.

As I said in the Introduction to this book, project management is a tough job, but it's also enormously rewarding and critically important. I applaud you for investing your time in growing your personal management and leadership excellence. I know your success will continue to grow, and that your success and influence will positively impact all the people lucky enough to work with you.

Please keep in touch with me through my website, *www.ProjectLeadershipGold.com*. It is my pleasure and privilege to serve, support, and enable you however I can.

Next Step:

Implement
Own the Forest, Delegate the Trees!

Now that you have the core concepts and essential "how-tos" of world-class project leaders, the next step is to obtain the full value by applying this information within your projects – to actually see and do things differently, and realize better results:

- *Where do you start?*
- *What do you apply first?*
- *Which change in your mindset and/or tactical performance will give you, your team and your company the biggest bang for the buck?*

If you would like powerful support to speed up your learning and implementation curve, Project Leadership Gold offers custom training, coaching, and success measurement and tracking programs that will help you apply this information - and more - in the easiest, most effective way possible.

- *Our programs respect the fact that you are probably working overtime already.*
- *Our programs help engage the internal management support you need to make the changes you know are most important.*

Invite the people in your company who can make the decision to invest in your performance, to give us a call and schedule a free 20-minute consultation to learn about the business value to them of investing further in you.

www.ProjectLeadershipGold.com

You can also purchase additional copies of Own the Forest, Delegate the Trees to share with your team. The more people know about your role and your challenges, the better they will be able to support you and do their part. Contact us for special bulk discount pricing.

Index

9-step 12,224

% 6,7,21,23,24,25,29,32,52,59,60,61,68,69, 71,78,81,82,83,84,108,131,168,183,188

A

Academic 195

Accountability 4,7,10,17,18,33,39,40,41,54, 55,64,78,81,82,94,99,101,115,124,125,127, 135,145,153,157,163,165,182,184,188,198, 201,210,232,235

Acknowledge 21,44,71,145,152,153,156, 186,216

Action
log 203,204,209
plan 203

Actual
realized data 62-63,84,110,238,245,248

ad-hoc
communications 242,246,249
meetings 59,60,70,86,205,213,214

Administration
assistant 4,214-215,217-218,231
portfolio 38
project management 3,4,33,57

Advice
from Barb 57,96,173,177,184
within team 43,49,141

Advisor 31,43-46,114,162,172,173, 236,238,242

Advisory Board 18,19,43-45,132,197,200

Agenda
meeting 126,127,156,203-204
personal 82

Agent 109,124,137,140,182,229

Aggressive 104,107,123,183,187-188

Agile 214,230

Agreement 19,20,24,39,46,56,60,62,76,86, 101,105,106,114,115,116,134,135,160,164, 165,181,183,184,197,202,209,228,233,238, 239,241

Albert Einstein 99

Allocation 24-25,28,42,59,60,61,62,71,81, 83,105,107,110,114,123,180,197,210,230, 238,239,252

Alternative 22,48,51,59-62,78,106-108,111, 114-116,182,187,197,206,230,235,238

Analyst
(see also Business Analyst)
(see also Programmer)
(see also Technical Lead Analyst)
personality type 154,156
technical 63,81,85

Andersen Change Management 143

Apollo 13 176

Approach
to consultants 50
to due dates 104
to keeping resources 181
to people 147,155
to project 51,86,95,114-117,195,206,213, 214,230-232,237,252

Approval 22,37,40,57,58,67,73,95,108,114, 115,123,140,147,183,186,213,219,221,230, 231,233,236-237,238-240,241-242,244-245, 248,251

Architecture 56,168,221

"as is" 63,236

Assessment
performance 25,77-78,186,201
self 170

Assumptions
about people 149-153,156,243
project 105,111,114,116,197,214,231,235
roles 9,16-17,19-21,41,82

Audience 67,93,112-115,147,159,162,167,
219-220,240

Authority
hire, fire 16,184
PM 17,55,70,111,125,127,141,197

Availability
resources 33,42,49,59-62,70,100,180,217,
234,243,251

Average
PM performance 6-7
project 7,55

B

BA
(see Business Analyst)

Barb 57,100,153,175

Barriers 10,128,145

Benefit 22,40,4-47,55,57-58,
113-114,142

Best Practice 38,51,87

Big Picture 3,5,8,11,68-69,72,77,88,
105-106,111,151,190,213,232,249

Blanchard, Ken 157

Bottom Line 18,57

Bottom-Liners 154-156

BPM
(see Business Program Manager) 42

Brainstorm 56,68-70,105,154,156,170,174,
176,181,207,229,236,252

Briefing 5,37,111-117,147,154,196-197,
219-220,230-231,234,236,238-239,240,
242

Budget 4,7,10,12,21,33,38,42,44,129,174,
179,197,210,235,238,245,248,252

Business hat 109,115

Business Analyst
mastermind team 85,87
operation processes 48,64-66,72
qualities 79,81-82
responsibilities 63,244
role nuances 19,23,63-66,68,69-71,202

Business Case 22,37

Business context 63,110,113,197

Business need 4,39,107,110-111,113,137,
174,197,246

Business People
typically 15,243
understanding 19-21,64,67-68,71-72

Business Process Implementers 23,71-72,
86,87

Business process redesign
(see Business process reengineering) 98

Business Program Manager 42,48

Business process reengineering 31,65,
86-87,213

Index 263

C

Calendar 44,205,218

Call to action 112,114,168

Canfield Jack Acknowledgments, 92,93,157

Carnegie Mellon Software Engineering Institute 39,99

Carnegie, Dale 39,99

CEO 132,134

CFO
(see Chief Financial Officer)

Champion 40

Change
Change Acceptance Curve 143-145
Change management 7-8,10,40,46-49,86, 64-66,71-72,79-80,85-87,110,139-140, 142,163,169,192,195,212-214,231,243, 244-245,249,251
resistance to 40,139-147

Charts
change acceptance curve 143
communication basics 166
governance 110
issues log 129
meeting calendar 205
negotiations 117
personality types 154-155
PM skills matrix 162
PM vs line manager 65
project management 11,121,226
project organization 29
project plan 198
project schedule 94,199
project vs program 30
program organization 32
resource trend 61,84
rolling agenda 203
tier concept 28

Checklist 12,206,224-253

Chief Financial Officer 45

Christopher Reeve 8

CMM 38

Coach 38,51,88,192

Coffee 18,70,177

Commitment
characteristic 82,91,95,98-99,102,135,147, 152,164-165,170,177,180,188-190,202, 235,238,246
resource 82-84,135,161,233,241,243

Common sense 24,39,88,98,108,126,206
(see also Issues)
due date 104
general 11,120-122,225
issue resolution 123-129
resources 33,59,71,75,183-184

Communications 15,19
executives, to 17,22,28,32,40-41,43-44, 63,66,80,85,87,111,118,155,157,161-171, 183,185,188-189,196,200-201,227,229, 236,242,249
Jack Canfield story 92,93
practices/structure 4,17,28,32,50,58,63,65, 72,91,97,101,111,118,122,126-128,140, 142,144-147,161-171,183,188-189, 195-196,200-201,214,217,220,229,239, 242,246,248-249,251-252
within the team 4,17,28,32,50,58,63,65,72, 91,97,101,111,118,122,126-128,140,142, 144-147,161-171,183,188-189,195-196, 200-201,214,217,220,229,239,242,246, 248-249,251-252
"you'll do it" story 6

Company grapevine 78

Competition 163

Compliance 101,168

Conflict 134,160

Consensus 134-135,207

Consequences 8,167-168

Constituent 57,58,122,132,136,161,163,167, 170,183,197,200,242

Constraints 41,68,105,167,179-186,196,227, 228,235,246

Consultants
 management of 49-51,69,173,207,227,230
 project roles 29,31,49,69,81,86,200

Context, business 63,110,113,197

Conversation, sample 100

Cost 7,22,37,47,55,63,103-105,110,114,165, 168,218,252

Creatives 155-156

Credit Card Service Corporation 85-86

Cruise, Tom 42

Cuba Gooding, Jr 42

Culture 7-8,24,55,131-137,188,191,227

Customer 4,48,71,79,86,87,142,163,213, 227,243,248

D

Dale Carnegie 39,99

Deadline
 (see also Due Date) 12,21,55,59,129,133, 135,145,157,181

Decision
 Maker 22,37,39,40,86,124,133-34,137,140, 182,239-240,251
 Package 37,228

Dedicated resources 76,81,84,86

Delegation
 Delegate the Trees 3-5,7,40,48,87,149,153
 the trees, defined 4
 mastermind mechanism 87
 within team 17-18,25,31,33,42,49,63,66, 67,71,87-88,95,123,141,149,153,157,163, 165,202,207,215-217,234

Deliverable 22,37,40,50,58,64,84,91,96, 97,111,124,126,128,135,141,145,153, 163-164,184,199-201,218,226,227-229, 230,233,236,238,241,244,248,251

Dependencies 85,96-98,105,140,180,251

Design
 (see also Redesign)
 (see also Requirements)
 business process 58,63,71-72,236,244-247
 general 28,56,64,65,85,109,144,156,183, 201,213,221,236,241,244-247,248,250
 team organization 30-33,85,88
 technical systems 56,67,72,168,236, 244-247

Developers 23,54,63,67,73,162

Doers
 defined 28-33
 roles & responsibilities 35,49,53-73,197, 201

Drivers
 defined 28-33
 roles & charts 35-51,53,132,200-201,227, 244,246

Index

Due date
expectations 11,39,42,55,113,153,164-165, 168,181-183,231,241
management of 23,49,50,55,73,94-97, 103-108,113,116,126,127-128,147,153, 164-165,168,181-183,187-191,199,209, 213,216,229,231,239,241,245,246,248,249
unrealistic 7,17,22,55

Dynalectron 174-175

E

Einstein, Albert 99

Emperor's New Clothes 118,137

Environment 39,65,149,157,251

Escalation 40,45,86,124,127-129,164,200, 205,242,245

Estimate 5,97,104,151,154,168,188,210, 214,221,229,250

Evaluate
(see also Assessment)
analyze 110,137,206,207
project performance 65,251-252,110,113, 206
team performance 112,117,184-185

Executives
(see also Briefing)
(see also Advisor)
(see also Negotiations)
(see also Communications)
(see also Decision-maker)
decisions 17,41,133,145,168,188-189,197, 210,211,237,238-240
role 18,21,38,40,42,43,47,49,132,133,136, 188-189,228,232
Survey of 6,9,55

F

Facilitate 125,127,174,176,204,207,209, 235-236,245

Facts 50,58,61,82,116,118,142,145-146,150, 153,155-156,159,164-166,181-182,200, 210-213,235-236,240,247

Fail 12,22,40,55,59,72,83,96,99,104,106, 132,141,143,146-147,152,167,183,191,202, 218,243

Fear 66,135,142,146-147,167,240

Feedback 18,45,134-135,141,159,216

Ford, Henry 99

Forest
(see Own)

Freddie Mac 79,80,86-87

G

Game 3,56,76,82,98,109,111,116,123,136, 144,180,228,234,244

Gaps 6,46,78,80,82,113,125,137,157,159, 161,164,181,206,236

Gartner 7,55

Generalizations
(see also Rule of Thumb)
(see also Guidelines)
broad 16,65

Goal
(see also Objectives)
business 6,109,144,227
general 15,42,133,167,170,183,235
project 9,10,27,94,144,196,227,235

Gooding, Cuba Jr 42

Governance 18,19,21,36-37,40,110,168,200

Grapevine, company 78

Graphics
(see Charts)

Guide
(see also Coach)
coach, counsel 9,33,51,67,73,79,88,207, 225,239

Guidelines 16,24,39,57,101,170,209,225

Gut 77-78,184-185,228

H

Hanks, Tom 133,176

Hat 19,21,56-57,109,115,245

Henry Ford 99

High-level 10,40,46,67,76,94,113-114,117, 144,183,187,198,219,225,228-230,231, 234,244-245

Hilton Hotels 97,98

Howard, Ron 176

I

Illustrations
(see Charts)

Implement
(see also Plan, Implementation)
business process 48,58,64,65,72,83,85, 142,195
intra-project process 38,65,72,87,91-92,101, 109,121,122,124,144,169,183,200,204, 206,213,214,231,238-242,244-245, 248-249,251-252

project 8,9,10,28,46,54,55,56,58,81,85, 87,97,108,114,139,200,206,208,212, 238-242,248,251-252

Implementer
(see Business Process Implementers)

Inertia 188

Influence acknowledgements,8,17-18,24, 29,43,47,86,88,112,117,124,132-134,163, 169,217,227,257

Information Technology 7,16,175,251

Inspire 8,169-170,196,229,245,249

Interim
deliverable 22,50,58,124,126,135,199
due date 58,94,144-145,189,242

Issues
(see Table of Contents)

IT
(see Information Technology)

IT leads
(see also Technical Lead Analyst) 68-69,191

IT People
(see also Technical People) 21-23,67-69, 243

J

Jack Canfield Acknowledgments, 92,93,157

Jerry Maguire 42

K

Ken Blanchard 157

Kickoff 76,197,234,239

Index

L

Leadership 3,9
described 3-10,132-136,227
skills, traits 31,55,59,66,81-82,85-87,100,
157-158,160,165,169-170,227,229,237,257
strategies 5,39,64,66,81,91,93,105-106,
132-136,165,169,188,205,213,227,229,230,
234,242

Level
(see also High-Level)
plan 96-98,144,183,187,190,198-199,230

Leverage 55,66,87

Lifecycle
chart 110,113,121
project 12,41,109,110,113,121,142,225

Line Manager
as stakeholders 45-48,64
business process implementers 71-72
described/about 16,23-25,64,66,82,181-182
performance input 24-25,82-83
vis a vis project manager 65,82-83,181

Location 140,213,220

Log
(see also Action Log)
document 197,230
issue log 125-129,218

Logistics 140,195,218

Lose
a resource 83,180-183
general 83,108,111,140,151,159

M

Machiavelli, Niccolo' 139

Manage
(see also Leadership) 10,11,12,23,25,28,30,
33,36-37,43,46,54,59,75,86-87,95,97,118,
121-122,123-124,127,134,135,139,
142-146,163,166-169,173,180,186,191,
196,198,202,218,220,225,230,235-236,
242-243,244-247,248-250,251-252

Management
(see also Change)
issue 124
other 22,31,46,49-51,63,73,78-79,81,85,
86,96,114,128,143,161,207,216,218,221,
257
project 5-10,12,19,31,33,38,43,49,55-58,
64-65,67,72,86,97,98,104,108,111,121,
128,149-153,163-164,169,177,182,195,
198,204,220,225,229,232,243,246,249,257
program 33,38,150-153
program office (PMO) 38-42,101,142,
200,202

Manager
(see also Line Manager)
(see also Project Manager)
(see also Program Manager)
One Minute 157
Other 18,42,45-49,67,78,140,157,161,
184-186,191-192,233,241,242-243

Master
contact list 207-208,218
project manager 6-7,171,196

Mastermind 85-88,163

Matrix
(see also Resources) 16,23-25,46,73,76,
82-86,182,184-185,214

Measure
37,38,40,55,62,65,180,192,212,214,220,
238,252

Meeting
calendar 205
casual 44-45
facilitation 207
issue resolution 125-129,242
minutes 203,209

Mentor 7,38,49,51

Methodology 3,5,31,38,63,98,195-196,206, 221,250

Microsoft 20,64,96,97,128,205,218

Mission 8,40,109,124-125,136137,147,162, 176,186,188,197

Monitor 24,38,55,65,125,127,184,196,198, 203,238,245,248,251

Mulcahy, Rita 221

N

Needs
(see Business need)

Negotiations
briefing 111-115,197,236
chart 117
how to 11,22,24,32-33,39,45,80-81,101, 104,105,106,109-118,133,174,179, 181-184,187,197,200,215,218,220,230, 236,238-240,248
project plan, due date 22,24,105,174,187, 197,220,238-240
resources 28,22,33,80-81,179,181-184, 218,230

Nelson Rockerfeller 99

Niccolo' Machiavelli 139

O

Objectives
project 4,32,33,40,43,76,104,113,136,160, 163,196,197,200,227,230,244
project manager 32,33,40,70,77,85,106,163, 196,226,227,230-231,233-234,235,238, 241,244,248,251

Obstacles 8,9,12,100,105-106,123,137,146, 151,154,187,190-191,195,227,229,231, 237,249

One Minute Manager
Meets the Monkey, The 157

One-on-one 44,76,199,228,237

Organization
chart 28,29,32,200-201
other/company 8,10,22,28,38-40,46-47,53, 65,77,92,124,133,134,140,165,173,248
project 15,18,27,28,29,31,33,35,53,71,76, 79,81,88,114,125,144,151,200-202,218,231
program 28,31-32,35,53,71

Own
Own the Forest, Delegate the Trees 3-5,7, 40,48,149,153
Own the Forest 3-5,7,40,55-56,48,149,153
The forest defined 4
Ownership, concept expanded 22,41,55-56, 72,95-96,152,190,196,202,204,232,239, 241,251

P

Peaceful Wisdom 144-145

Percent
(see %)

Performance
(see also Assessment)
personnel 23-23,78,83,170,184,192,252
project 137,192,214,220

Personal Relationships 45-47,78-79,132, 135,137,169-171,208,216,241

Personalities 63,82,137,146,149-160,170, 188,216

Personnel 38,65,86-87,125,184,202,246

Phase
chance acceptance 143-144
project 59-63,67,86-87,94-98,114,174,180, 183,199-201,213,229,230-231,233-234, 241,245-246,249,251

Index

Plan
detailed 95-98,180,202-203
implementation 231,238-240,242,251
project 22,38,45,55,73,85,92,95-108,114,
126,128,150,167,169,179-180,184,
187-189,197-203,213-214,218,220,230,
238,244,248,252
resource 20,75-88,183,184,214,238
strategic 70

PM
(see Project Manager)

PMI 221

PMO
(see Project Management Office)

Point person 32,42,48,67,128,142

Policies 36,65,71,139,163,221

Politics 4,45,66,131-134,227,240

Portfolio Management 38,221

Power 5,17-18,43,51,55,58,64,69,82,85,95,
96,111,131-132,140,142,146,151,174-176,
200,213

Powerpoint 17,41,219-220

President 46,132

Pressure 95,145,180,187-191,211,245

Principles of Success, The 92,175

Priority 23,25,42,43,47,51,62,73,82,84,110,
127,128,131-132,136-137,150,163,168,
180,196,207,215,218,236,252

Proactive 4,95,123,131,135,146,164,167,
196,205,239,245,248

Problem
(see also Issues)
people 150-151
solving 4,73,86,94,204-206

Procedures 36,65,71,91,101,221,238

Process
(see also Issues)
(see also Problem solving)
(see also Negotiations)
business 31,63-65,69,71-72,82,86,169,
212-213,243,244-245,248
interview 78
operational 46,48,65
triage 124,127

Process Implementers 23,71-72,86,87

Program
(see also Organization)
defined 27,43
management office 38-42,101,142,200,202
manager 32-33,38,42-43,49
organization chart 32
organization strategies 30-34
versus project 27,30,43

Programmer
(see Developers)

Progress 4,8,17,24,32,37-38,45,50,80,84,97,
125,153,188,196-197,200,205,214,215,236,
238-239

Project
(see also Organization)
(see also Manage)
defined 9
governance 18,19,21,36-37,40,110,168,200
organization chart 29
organization strategies 31,33-34
portfolio management 38,221
schedule 62,92,94-95,114,183,199-200,218
versus program 27,30,43

Project Manager
defined 10
general 3,5-6,9,10,12,16,22-23,36,41,54-58,
   65,73,81,95,104,107,121,124,171,184,
   191-192,195,215,225,242,253,257
technical 56-58,73
vis a vis line management 64-66

Project Leadership
(see also Leadership)
defined 3,9

Project Lifecycle 12,41,109,110,113,121,
142,225

Project Management
(see also Management)
a game 56
chart 11
defined 9
vis a vis line management 65

Project Management Institute 221

Project Plan
(see Plan)

Promotion 24,140,161

Q

Quality 10,38,55,78,154,168,185,201,207,
246

Quantify 47,98,179,185

Quality Assurance 38

R

Recommendations
from you to others 19,37,39,106-108,
   111-116,137,197,210,219,235-237,
   238-240,252
to you as PM 20,25,35,51,53,72,77,79,142,
   150,157-159,170,176,207,211-212,253

Re-engineering
(see Business process re-engineering)

Redesign
(see Business process reengineering) 98

Reeve, Christopher 8

Relationship
(see also Roles & Responsibilities)
issues 41,45,132,146,179
personal 45,149-160,169-171,185-186
reporting 25,197,200-201,243
strategies 3-5,15-18,24,27,35,44,47,51,
   53,69,76,85,133-134,140,149-160,163,170,
   185-186,200-201,227-228,232,233,237,243

Report
(see Briefing)
(see Status)

Requirements
business 46,54,58,63,67,69,72,87,221,244,
   248,251
executive 43,46
project 20,39,40-43,221,251
technical 56,248

Resent 100,146-147,190

Resistance 40,91,100,135,139-147,155,250

Resources
(see also Allocation)
(see also Commitment)
(see also Common sense)
(see also Constraints)
(see also Matrix)
(see also Negotiations)
(see also Plan)
(see also 'Sufficiency')
analytical 133-234
communication roles 92-94
implementation 239,241-243
initiation 76
issues 179-180,185,242
lose a 83,180-183

Index

matrix 25,82,84
mix 22,56
negotiations for 22,46-47
shortfalls 60-63
SME challenges 59-63
trend chart 61

Resource Planning
(see also Resources)
challenge 75
committed versus received 83-84
Freddie Mac example 79-80
lead role quality chart 82
objective 77
overview 20,76-88,183-184
PM questions 76
steps 79
strategy session 77-79
Sufficiency of resources 75-84
time allocation 81-84

Responsibilities
(see Table of Contents)

Results
(see also Target)
(see also Measure)
business 42,66,192,252
project 18,72

Reviews
(see Approval)
(see Performance)

Right Hand 69-71,228

Risk 39,47,55,78,95,101,106,110,128,131,
135,182-183,187,190-191,202,212,214,216,
228,229,231,247

Rita Mulcahy 221

Roadblocks 69

Rockerfeler, Nelson 99

Rocky 257

Roles & Responsibilities
(see Table of Contents)
communicate 92-94
Jack Canfield Story 92-94

Rolling agenda 127,203-204

Rollout 10,54,72,248,249,251,252

Ron Howard 176

Root 164-166

Routine
(see Table of Contents) 91-92

Rules of thumb
(see also Generalizations) 68,81,95,151,202

S

Salary 23-25,83

Sarbanes-Oxley 38

Schedule
chart 94,199
project 62,92,94-95,114,183,199-200,218

Scope
manage 49,64-66,69,71,77,113,170,174,
183,227,238,246
negotiate 22,105-107,113-116,183,187,
238-239

SEI 39

Self-assessment
(see Assessment)

Skill assessment
(see Performance) 77-79

SME
(see Subject Matter Expert)

Software 38,55,96,179,214,221,231,248,250

Solution
(see also Alternative)
design 63,65
technical 56,67-69,244

Sponsor
advisory board 44-45
effectively engage 17-19
governance board 37
responsibilities 40
SME challenges 59-63
typically 16
understanding 16-17,40-43
all references 6-7,12,16-19,22,29,37,39-49,
  55,61-62,66,76,86-87,104-107,110-117,
  129,132-134,137,142-145,147,151,162,
  166-167,170,182,185,187-188,192,197,
  199-202,210-213,216-217,227,229,
  230-232,234,236-239,242,244-245,251-252

Stakeholder
business process implementers 71-72
defined 42,45-46
operations management 48
resources, matrixed 46-47
SME challenges 59-63
vis a vis line management 64-66
all references 18-19,25,37,42-43,45-48,62,
  64,66,72,76,82,86,112,114,129,132,145,
  151,162,167,182,197,200,227,229-231,
  233-234,241-245

Standish Group, The 7

Statistics
(see also %)
about project management 7,42,55
labor, Bureau of 49

Status
contains 17,169,191,198,210-213
produce 17,38,64,169,191,198,204,210-213,
  218,242

Step
by step 92,155-156
into 15,24,35,53,191,232,248
next 114,147,216,225,229,233,237
nine 12,224-253
up 3,18,55,66,111,135,137,184,188,211,243

Story 47,61,112,115-116,155,165,197,219

Strength 8,33,63,78,106,158-160,169

Structure
(see also Organization)
management of 62,246,249
organization 15,18,29,31-32,88,133,200-201
project 64,92,250
routine and 91-101
thinking & analysis 235-236

Subject Matter Expert (SME)
about 54,57-64,66,68-69,71-72,80-81,87,
  162,168,244-245
business process implementers 71-72
challenges 59
responsibilities 58

Sufficiency
of resources 75-80
strategy session 77-80

Survey 6-7

Systems
(see also Process)
analyst 85
technical 86,212-213,244-245,248

T

Target
(see also Goal)
due date 113,168,199
results 4,7,9,21,37,58,113,227,244,252

Tasks
(see Plan, project)

Index 273

Team
business 12
effective 10,11,13,88
executive 107
implementation 213,238,241
incoming 15-25
leadership 132,135-136,234,242
mastermind 85-88
members 15,20,24-25,50-51,81,83,91,93, 103,135,147,179,184,188-189,197,201,205, 207,213,217,233,241,246,249
technical 12,85
thrown-together 75

Technical Lead Analyst
(see also IT Leads)
lead role quality chart 82
mastermind team 86
responsibilities 67
role nuances 67-69,69-71

Technical People
(see also IT people)
(see also Technical Lead Analyst)
in business sessions 67-69
technical PM message 56-58
typically 15
understanding 21-23

Techniques
facilitation 207
other 5,50,66,104,192,230,237,257

Technology 7,16,56-57,67,174-175,251

Template 38

Test
plan 63,250
project activity 28,54,56,58,63-65,71-72, 85,168,183,248,250

Threat 4,39,129,135,151,168,180,203,247

Tier Concept 28

Time allocation 24,71,81-84,180

Timeline 22,62,76,82,104,116,127-128,168, 202,210

Tip 35,73,156,192,207,220,225,242,257

"to be" 63,65,69,236

Tom Cruise 42

Tools
and Logistics 195-221
and Methodology 38,50-51,195-196,221

Tom Hanks 133,176

Total Quality Management 207

TQM 207

Training 38,48,63-65,71-72,85,87,170,183, 192,207,214,243,248

Transettlements 175

Trees
defined 4
delegate the 3-5,7,40,48,87,149,153

Trend 61-62

Triage 124,127

Trust 18-19,78,82,85116-117,146,151-152, 164,170,176,185,191,231

U

Urgent 76,91,95-98,113,137,147,153,162, 188-189,217,233,241

V

Valley of Despair 143-144

Value proposition 108-111,113

Variables
 lists of 106,131
 types of communication 166

Virtual 214

Vision 3,5,40,58,118,143-144,147,162-163, 188,196-197,237,240

Voicemail 142,210,216-217

W

War room 213-214, 231

Weakness 33,106,158-159,169

Workaround 84,165

Y

Y2K 97